Stirring a conviction that is deep,
resolute, and enduring

CONVICTION

Troy Fitzgerald

Produced by the
General Conference of Seventh-day Adventists®
Youth Ministries Department

Adventist
Youth Ministries

Primary contributor: Troy Fitzgerald

Layout and design: Lauren Heinrich, Jessica Coffee

Cover design: Jessica Coffee

Editorial work: Faith Hoyt, Meghann Heinrich, Lauren Heinrich, Cameron Fitzgerald

Senior Editorial Assistant: Vanessa Correa

All definitions are from the *Merriam-Webster's Collegiate Dictionary*, Tenth Edition.

CONVICTION

Rights for publishing this book outside the U.S.A. or in non-English languages are administered by the Youth Ministries Department of the Seventh-day Adventist® Church. For additional information, please visit our website, www.gcyouthministries.org, email Youthinfo@ gc.adventist.org, or write to Youth Ministries Department, General Conference of Seventh-day Adventists® Church, 12501 Old Columbia Pike, Silver Spring, MD 20904, U.S.A.

Library of Congress Cataloging-in-Publication Data

Names: Fitzgerald, Troy, 1968- author. | General Conference of Seventh-Day Adventists. Youth Ministries Department.
Title: Conviction : stirring a conviction that is deep, resolute, and enduring / Troy Fitzgerald.
Description: Nampa : Pacific Press Publishing Association, 2018. | Produced by the General Conference of Seventh-day Adventistsª Youth Ministries Department.
Identifiers: LCCN 2018014066 | ISBN 9780816363674 (pbk. : alk. paper)
Subjects: LCSH: Youth—Religious life. | Young adults—Religious life. | Youth—Prayers and devotions. | Young adults—Prayers and devotions. | Bible—Devotional use.
Classification: LCC BV4531.3 .F548 2018 | DDC 242/.6—dc23 LC record available at https://lccn.loc.gov/2018014066

FOREWORD

Conviction is a biblical conversation about our deepest values and core assumptions. In the last twenty-five years, I have endeavored to engage young adults about embracing the call to follow Christ and join the ranks of witnesses—people who live *with* God instead of just knowing *about* God. I focused on the question of what it means to mature in Christ. The Seventh-day Adventist Church has poured so much effort into helping children grow in their faith; but the transition to owning their faith, handing off the baton, seems less successful. Because I love the Savior, His church, and this wonderful work, I became passionate about the process of ownership in God's family.

Years of research and experiences with young adults have helped us develop a fifty-two-week devotional format. In our conversations and planning for this project, we have discovered that the practices and rhythms of young adult life require a simple approach. Many use devotions as the prompt for Bible studies, small groups, dialogues, and discussions for social media. But mostly, they just want one thought to practice throughout the week so they can deepen their experience with God.

I hope and pray you will not have devotions anymore. Keep reading. Before you edit this sentence or start a new controversy. Hear me out. Instead of having devotions, *be devoted*. Take the *s* off the end of *have devotions* and go with *have devotion*. *Conviction* is about having devotion and much more.

The daily concept is still valuable today and is a time-tested tradition in Adventist history, but the weekly approach seems to resonate with young adults. When I asked about their feelings regarding a daily devotional, they responded, "With all the things we have to do every day, it feels like homework. The weekly approach allows us to steep in the Word of God rather than sample the ideas."

With this in mind, here is the format you will discover in this devotional:

- Each chapter has been chosen by young adult believers. In retreats, we spend the weekend scouring the Word of God to find the best examples for discussion.

- Each chapter's theme prompts the thoughts and actions of the reader.

- Each chapter has suggestions for application throughout the week.

- Each chapter contains extra passages of scripture for those who want further reflection small groups and personal Bible study.

In other words, *Conviction* is a young adult devotional from scripture that prompts the participant to enjoy the Word throughout week. These pages are for you. Know that this church loves you. It understands the big decisions you are making in this season of life. You can be sure that through His Word, God will make His will clear. Rest in His love and lead with conviction and grace.

CONTENTS

BEYOND BELIEF 57

OF CONSCIENCE & CONFIDENCE 79

FULLY ASSURED 97

KINGDOM CONVICTIONS 109

INTRODUCTION

The quest of young adults for conviction is a process of learning how to combine the mind and the heart with action. While some have firm opinions and even personal beliefs, a conviction compels you to live differently. In other words, there are things you *can* do, *want* to do, and *should* do, but a conviction is something you feel you *must* do.

What truth do you believe rises to the level of conviction? What cause moves you to risk ending a relationship? What action is so necessary in the world today that you would spend yourself to see it succeed? Name the virtue that you are unashamed to display in public or the quality you work persistently to shape your character, even if doing so moves you out of your comfort zone. Although the word "conviction" does not appear in the Bible very often, the evidence of people who live according to conviction is common in scripture. In this book you will see how conviction stirs, builds, and changes a life. All over the world, young adults yearn to commit their lives to what is convincing.

Biblical conviction is refined in the fire of effort, failure, faith, and hope. Even though conviction is a matter of the heart, it is often displayed on your sleeve. Some themes that you will encounter in this book are rich insights into human nature and the rules of the heart. You will meet biblical people stirred to their core by conviction. As you read, consider the relationship between the Holy Spirit, the conscience, and the person you are called to be. Take this journey and discover how you can be resolute, sure, and confident in your faith.

HEART BURN

There is a lot of talk about the heart. Is it an organ? Is it the mind? Does thinking with your heart mean completely disconnecting from a coherent thought process? When all are called to "love God with all your heart, soul, and mind" how does this occur? Why are some ideas so important to some believers and not so much to others? Are convictions more like "love at first sight" or do they tend to be born out of commitment and sacrifice? How is it that our hearts can be so unreasonably passionate and so surprisingly inconsistent? Conviction is a matter of the heart, but see how the heart works according to God's great design.

1. SENSE ABLE

"Therefore we do not lose heart... For our light and momentary troubles are achieving for us an eternal glory that far outweighs them all. So we fix our eyes not on what is seen, but on what is unseen, since what is seen is temporary, but what is unseen is eternal."
(2 Corinthians 4:16-18)

Conviction begins and ends with the heart. Whether it is a truth you love or an idea you learn to love, your conviction grows the more you commit your heart to action. For example, if you deeply believe that followers of Christ must defend and protect those who are vulnerable, then your belief only strengthens as you practice it. It is also true that when you don't exercise your conviction, your heart eventually weakens in its fervor. In other words, the core beliefs of the heart never remain static, but ebb and flow with practice or neglect. Think about the landscape of your convictions through the years and identify seasons when your passions soured, and new ideas became sweet. If you reflect long enough, you may recall truths you had a heart for, but the passion eventually faded. You are not alone.

"Therefore we do not lose heart."

How? How do you keep growing? How do you thrive? How do you win when everything around you seems to be failing? It seems as if every time you take a step forward life knocks you back two steps. Problems afflict you. Financial trouble assails you. Work discourages you. Relationships devastate you. Disease threatens you. Sickness weakens you. And death... well, death waits for you. If you use your five senses, they all echo you the same basic message: don't expect much and you won't be disappointed. It is futile to try. Joy is destined to end. Everything new gets old. If good happens, then the bad is just around the corner.

The apostle Paul is swift to curb despair into hope by saying, "If you want to grow your heart, deepen your belief, and strengthen your conviction, you must learn to be *sense able*." Intentionally activate a new way of seeing, feeling, tasting, touching, and hearing. Paul explains further, saying, "So we fix our eyes not on what is seen, but on what is unseen."

To "fix our eyes" is not simply an attempt to keep one's attention from drifting or restrain the mind from chasing distractions. To "fix your eyes" is to know when to cover your ears and look instead of listen. Sometimes it even means you close your eyes and trust that God hears you even though you can't see Him. To "fix your eyes" is not a commitment to only use the sense of vision; it's about purposing the mind to see more than what eyes alone can see. Examine your heart today. What are the truths that you can know even with your eyes closed? Living by faith is not walking through this life blind, ignorant, and disconnected from the world around us. Fixating on the eternal is the way to set your heart on eternal things first and foremost.

INSIDE OUT

What is your strongest sense? Smell? Taste? Sight? Touch? Hearing? If you had to live without one of your senses, which would you choose to give up? Even with the knowledge that your brain can reconfigure pathways to compensate for the loss, it would be difficult to make that choice. Reflect and share your response.

Think about this process: Convictions are non-negotiable beliefs that run deep in the heart/mind. When your ideas become actions, and actions produce experiences, and ultimately those experiences become values to live by. Think about how this process describes the way your convictions have come into being.

We tend to see what we are looking for. Look at your immediate surroundings for anything that is red. Did you notice how easy it was to identify red items because you set your mind to do so? While it may not be as easy as seeking out a color, consider looking for a positive quality in a person or listening for the sound of encouragement and hope throughout the day. Also, practice looking for examples in your daily life that contrast the eternal versus the temporary.

Read and reflect on what the Bible says about spiritual vision.
- Psalm 19:8
- Matthew 6:22
- Matthew 13:15
- 1 Corinthians 2:9
- Ephesians 1:18
- Hebrews 12:2

2. SEARCH CONDITIONS

*"But from there you will seek the L*ORD* your God and you will find him, if you search after him with all your heart and with all your soul."*
(Deuteronomy 4:29)

The journey from childhood to adulthood is a road paved with many different commitments. Early in life children learn what they are good at and commit to developing skills to become even better. Later on youth commit to friendships that resonate with their ideas about who they are and who they want to be. As the journey continues, youth mature into adults as they are called upon to relate to God personally, intimately, and resolutely during a season when all of their choices seem to be pivotal. To fully commit *all to God* amid *all the other things they are expected to work on* is a challenge for many. However, if you want God, He wants *all of you*. Only those who *seek with all of their hearts* encounter an enduring life with their Creator. Just in case you are wondering what it really looks like to commit your all at the outset of the relationship, consider Christ, who led the way.

The story of the lost sheep and coin are a response to the Pharisees' complaint that Jesus "welcomed sinners and ate with them" (Luke 15:2). Is it any surprise that the owner of the sheep and the woman who lost the coin search *until* the find what they are looking for? Not when the owner of the sheep and the woman in the parable represent God's commitment to find lost people. The question is, "Does God expect the same kind of commitment from those who would seek Him?"

Reflect on the promises God made in the Old Testament to His followers: "I will make *all* your enemies turn their backs and run" (Exodus 23:27); "Before *all* your people I will do wonders never before done in any nation in all the world" (Exodus 34:10); "Worship the L*ORD* your God; it is He who will deliver you from the hand of *all* your enemies" (2 Kings 17:39); "…you will be clean from *all* your sins" (Leviticus 16:30; God's promise on the Day of Atonement); "I delivered you from the hand of *all* your oppressors" (Judges 6:9).

The condition of a full commitment is not some Old Testament tactic that has now become outdated or irrelevant. When curious disciples inquired about where He was going, Jesus replied, "Come and you will see" (John

1:39). If you were hoping to fully vet the teachings of Jesus before you choose to embrace them, then you might want to read John 7:17, where the Savior declares, "Anyone who chooses to do the will of God will find out whether my teaching comes from God or whether I speak on my own." Finally, the apostle Paul urges all seekers: "Offer your bodies as a living sacrifice, holy and pleasing to God—this is your true and proper worship... Then you will be able to test and approve what God's will is—his good, pleasing and perfect will" (Romans 12:1, 2). To some, this sequence of logic does not sound right, but the more you think about God's commitment to people, the more it starts to make sense.

When you search for God "with all your heart", it is not some arbitrary obstacle meant to make your relationship with God more difficult. God has always been the first one to fully commit. This is how He relates to the human family: "But God demonstrates His own love for us in this: while we were still sinners, Christ died for us" (Romans 5:8); "This is love: not that we loved God, but that He loved us and sent His Son as an atoning sacrifice for our sins" (1 John 4:10).

First. All. Then.

Those who stir with Christian conviction *first* place their lives in the Savior's hands. Those who live a life marked by joy, victory, and promise leverage *all* that they are for a genuine walk with God. According to Scripture, then *and only then* do seekers find what they are searching for. As you think about your relationship with God today, are you committed to pursue God with all of your heart and soul?

INSIDE OUT

As you reflect on your own journey with God, when did you come to the place where you understood that God wanted to have a personal relationship with you?

Often the things that get in the way or distract you from a close walk with God are not inherently evil or destructive, but they tend to seem equally important in the moment. What are some obstacles that get in the way of a full commitment to a life with God?

In your mind, survey through the Bible and identify people who fully committed their lives to God even though they did not have all the answers.

This week how will you organize your life to put your relationship with God first? What are specific choices that you will make?

3. ALL FOR LOVE

"'Of all the commandments, which is the most important?' ... 'Love the Lord your God with all your heart and with all your soul and with all your mind and with all your strength. The second is this: Love your neighbor as yourself. There is no commandment greater than these.'" (Mark 12:28-31)

Matthew, Mark, and Luke all tell the story of religious leaders testing Jesus on the question of the greatest commandment. Some people today recoil at the terms "command" or "law" or even the word "obey", because it somehow seems to convey an empty religious practice. Note that the answer Jesus gives does not begin with "Thou shall not..." but the word "love".

Now, think of all the things in life you love and make a list. I love chocolate, warm weather, and the color of amethyst. I love the smell of bread baking, my 30-year-old car, my soccer shoes, and the rich sound of a cello. I love my wife, my sons, and my barbecue recipe. I love the wind, the mountains, and paper plates that I don't have to wash. I love my friends, my dog, and Jesus.

Of course, this list is not ranked in any kind of order, but notice the range of things that get the label of being "loved". The point is sometimes the word is used so often that "love" can lose its luster. However, when Jesus replied, "Love the Lord" and "love your neighbor", He was selecting one verse from the Deuteronomy 6:5 and another from Leviticus 19:18. The Jews had a way of expanding the law and summarizing the commands to one sentence.

Isaiah 33:15 reduces all the law down to six simple statements and Micah 6:8 simplifies the law to three, saying, "Do justice, love mercy, and walk humbly with God." Read Isaiah 56:1 and the faithful prophet squeezed God's commands to two: "keep justice" and "do righteousness". However, Habakkuk 2:4 is the ultimate summary, declaring, "The righteous shall live by faith." John would take a lesson from the prophets of old and distill the gospel down to: "Whoever does not love does not know God, because God is love" (1 John 4:8).

It may be that some people crave well-crafted phrases and eloquent sentences that inspire and enlighten the mind. The point of asking people to summarize the law was to move people to wrestle with the word of God. Basically, it's one of the oldest teaching strategies in the book. The process of thinking, choosing, and distilling the law to a few important truths is how you come to own the message. Your own sense of conviction will stir the more you actively process God's truth for yourself.

Also, notice one final thought about this encounter in Mark 12:28-34. Even though three of the four gospels tell this story, each story is a little different. While Matthew and Luke describe the hostility between the Jewish leaders and Jesus, Mark tells the story showing a warm, appreciative encounter. After the teachers of the law heard how Jesus silenced the Sadducees, they simply shared back and forth until Jesus declares, "You are not far from the kingdom of God." May your love for God continue to find new ways to organize and express the truth you believe.

INSIDE OUT

Examine the three accounts of this story and note the way each perspective is different and how they all still portray the same event.
- Matthew 22:34-40
- Luke 10:25-37
- Mark 12:28-34
- Deuteronomy 6:1-9

Read Psalm 15:1-5 and notice how David tried to summarize the whole law in about five or six statements. Think about how you would condense the Ten Commandments to five one or two-word statements.

Paraphrase. Choose a handful of your favorite passages from Scripture and rewrite them, but don't use any of the words that are already used in the text. Of course, necessary words like to, and, the, and it are appropriate. The task of paraphrasing the Scripture in this way forces the reader to wrestle with what it means.

Read John 20:30, 31. Think about what John had to leave out and what he chose to include. Such a process might be one of the ways to discover what your core beliefs are. If you had to say who you are by telling five stories or events from your life, which five would you tell?

4. SOURCE OR SYMPTOM

"You brood of vipers, how can you who are evil say anything good? For the mouth speaks what the heart is full of. A good man brings good things out of the good stored up in him, and an evil man brings evil things out of the evil stored up in him." (Matthew 12:34, 35)

Do you agree or disagree with the following?

- You can listen to the words a person speaks and know a lot about the state of his or her heart.
- Mood, body language, and tone communicate the state of the heart more than words.
- There are some who, knowingly or unknowingly, can use words to disguise the true intent of their hearts.

Brain research continues to reveal the majesty of God's creative genius—even if some researchers don't believe a Creator is responsible. One particular finding relates to what Jesus said about the mouth and the mind (the heart): *What you think drives what you say, but saying what you think deepens the belief even more.*

The tendency is to silence words that are not helpful to you or those you find problematic. Countries that often oppress people will try to suppress the press, or any other organization that stirs the people in a direction the government does not value. With the passing of time, the rhetoric may quiet down, but eventually the hearts of the people will awaken with a loud voice. Have you ever tried to ignore a toothache? The pain is a constant distraction and you simply can't function well. Normal activities like going to school, work, having simple conversations, recreation, and even sleep are dominated by the throbbing pain in your mouth. If you just ignore it long enough, the pain will subside eventually and even seem to go away entirely, but when the body stirs the infection, the pain returns with even greater severity.

Imagine what the Christian church would be like if more careful attention were given to the heart that produces words. In Ephesians 4:29 Paul warns believers of the nature of words and how they can spread treachery, but also goodness: "Do not let any unwholesome talk come out of your mouths, but only what is helpful for building others up according to their needs, that it may benefit those who listen." James will agree that, "Everyone should be quick to listen, slow to speak and slow to become angry, because human anger does not produce the righteousness that God desires. Therefore, get rid of all moral filth and the evil that is so prevalent and humbly accept the word planted in you, which can save you" (James 1:19-21). Common to both passages is how the mind and the heart are the center and source of anything that is spoken.

Take a moment and try to remember the conversations you have had recently. If your conversations tend to be short and superficial, what does that say about your heart? Well, it doesn't mean you are superficial, but it does reveal how busy, or shy, or careful you might be. What if your words tend to find problems or things that are inconsistent or not helpful? Perhaps you know people who tend to see all the things that are broken. Part of this trait is the noble quality of being analytical. However, you may also observe that people who criticize more often than edify are wrestling in their hearts with more than meets the eye.

The same principle applies to what Jesus said about adultery. Jesus taught, "You have heard that it was said, 'You shall not commit adultery.' But I tell you that anyone who looks at a woman lustfully has already committed adultery with her in his heart" (Matthew 5:27, 28). The act of adultery is only the result of a duplicitous heart. To be sure, those who deepen in the core convictions are often people who recognize how keenly the heart is connected to what people say and do. No one is more familiar with the way of the heart than the One who designed it.

What is the condition of your heart today? Are the words you speak a window into your mind? May the grace that has been freely given to you make you ready to speak well to others this week.

INSIDE OUT

Reflect on the condition of your heart today. What do you often speak about and what do you often think about?

Choose an object or something tangible to remind you about the connection between your words and your heart.

Identify three people you interact with who tend to bring out the worst in your heart; plan to be more careful with your words and how you say them.

5. THE STATES OF THE HEART

"The seed on good soil stands for those with a noble and good heart, who hear the word, retain it, and by persevering produce a crop." (Luke 8:15)

Young adults who seek to live with conviction will ultimately be people who know their own hearts. Many today are fired up for a cause or may be activists in waiting, but have not thought long enough to connect to the source of their restlessness. In order to know what effort to give yourself to, you ought to first know the "you" that is to be given. The same is true when people prepare for marriage. There is a common assumption that really knowing the other person well is the secret to a happy home, when knowing yourself is more critical by far. Jesus repeatedly called for people to examine their own hearts, and when that didn't work, He told a story.

When you look at the stories Jesus told, some are short and open-ended. The message is obscure enough to hide the meaning from those who do not have good intentions and at the same time spark a thought for those who are tracking with the kingdom. Jesus explained this to His disciples when they asked, "Why do you speak to the people in parables?" He replied, "Because the knowledge of the secrets of the kingdom of heaven has been given to you, but not to them" (Matthew 13:10, 11). The message is less about an "us and them" mentality and more about the state of the human heart. The parable of the sower is one of those lessons that cause people to honestly examine the state of their hearts.

State of the Heart #1 "Those along the path…"
There are so many ways in which a person can shut his or her mind to God. The seed thrown on the path has no chance to grow because the way is closed. This particular heart condition may come about by prejudice, arrogance, pride, fear, or a selfish and immoral character. Whatever the reason, the seed will not take at all and the heart will not grow anything.

State of the Heart #2 "Those on the rocky ground…"
The rocky ground represents the heart that never really thinks things through. The soil is shallow. The phrase "easy come, easy go" captures the nature of this rock-cluttered soil. There is always room for change, but

rarely space for transformation. Commitments are made, but not kept. The state of such a heart cannot bear the scrutiny of intelligent thought or the quiet strength of roots that tunnel deep. The heart may initially grow "joyfully", but will not endure the heat of the day.

State of the Heart #3 "The seed that fell among thorns..."
For some life is filled with so many commitments and various "good" things to do. The crowded life has no room for prayer, no space for faithful service, and no area to stretch out in which the character can grow slowly. Instead of hearing God's voice in the word, the crowded, thorn-riddled heart only hears the alarms that signal the next thing to do. The seed that falls on the thorny ground is a heart so busy with competing demands that whatever grows will ultimately die.

State of the Heart #4 "The seed on good soil..."
Of course, the good soil is soft, weed-free, and rockless. And while you may want your heart to be described that way, it is likely that you identify more with the other soils. It's important to realize that good soil can still have a weed and a rock or two nearby, given the known fact that a garden requires continual work to keep the soil healthy.

If you decided to read this book, rest in the truth that your soil is good. There may be rocks, weeds, and a stubborn character that resists the impulse of the Spirit occasionally, but by God's grace your soil is good— good enough to examine it. It is the unexamined heart that is in the most danger. May the good news of Christ find a good place to grow in you today.

INSIDE OUT

This week, read and reflect on some passages about the state of the heart.
- Matthew 5:8
- Matthew 13:15
- 2 Corinthians 13:5
- Lamentations 3:40
- Ezekiel 18:27, 28

Find a place near your home where you can dig up some ground and examine the state of the ground. Pay attention to actual examples of this parable in the regular course of your week. Identify a few areas of your life that need to be weeded or removed. Pray about this and share with a friend the need to cultivate the soil of your heart more intentionally.

6. PRACTICE MAKES PERMEATE

"For where your treasure is, there your heart will be also." (Matthew 6:21)

Imagine a tea bag being lowered into the steaming water. The porous, netted bag contains fragments of leaf, small sinews of dried sticks and fibers crushed into small pieces, but not into powder. As the bag fully submerges, the water presses in around and steadily penetrates the barrier, seeping into the collection of herbal material. The heat and the water together permeate the tea flakes and soon even smaller particles ooze out of the bag in feathery wisps of color that look like plumes of smoke. Because of this beautiful process, more and more of the water transforms from clear to a rich brown color—when the water gets into the bag of tea, what is in the bag spills out into the water. Behold the great work of permeation.

Consider what it looks like in the flow of everyday living:
- When young people give their hard earned money to relieve the hunger and suffering of people they don't even know—permeation.
- When someone takes a moral stand for right in a culture that embraces wrong, experiencing scorn and ridicule as a result—permeation.
- When you dare to do the most unconventional and unimaginable act of forgiving your enemies and treating them with mercy it exhausts you, but restores your soul—permeation.
- When you can't see, feel, or sense God's existence, but decide to pray, read, and serve until He reveals Himself to you—permeation.

Convictions of the heart are not caught from the air as some great notion flies by. Ideas from sermons, books, or even moments that seem like epiphanies are all part of the work of inspiration, but there is more—much more. The most valuable ideas are not simply believed or things you agree with in your head, but they are cultivated as you practice them. To make something "your treasure" is to demonstrate its value. If you were stranded in the desert, how much would you pay for a bottle of clean water? The question is not "How much does it cost?", but "How much is it worth to you?" Jesus challenges believers to embrace the rule of permeation. Whatever you make valuable will inevitably have a place in your heart. Sometimes it is tempting to think that you must wait to give your heart to that which compels you or sells you. *According to Jesus, what you do faithfully will ultimately cause you to love it more fully.*

Think about how the Sermon on the Mount ends. Perhaps the greatest challenge Jesus gives to those who would follow Him comes in a series of practical, tangible things to do:
- Shine your light through good works. (Matthew 5:16)
- Do and teach God's commands. (Matthew 5:19)
- Be reconciled to your brother. (Matthew 5:24)
- Love and forgive your enemies like God does. (Matthew 5:43-48)
- Give, pray, trust, and cultivate heavenly treasure. (Matthew 6)
- Judge yourself first, then deliver help with mercy. (Matthew 7:1-6)
- Do the best for others. (Matthew 7:12)
- Choose to walk the narrow way. (Matthew 7:13,14)
- Be aware, use discernment, and know God personally. (Matthew 7:15-23)

The crowning statement Jesus makes is about hearing and doing what He calls you to do. "Therefore everyone who hears these words of mine and puts them into practice is like a wise man who built his house on the rock" (Matthew 7:24).

As you practice the great principles of God, they permeate your heart like hot water permeates a bag of tea. If you sit and wait for conviction to somehow stir in you, you will likely be on the couch indefinitely. The process of permeation is God's standard operating procedure. The more you avail yourself to Him, the more He gets into you. As you treasure God's truth in your life this week, know that heaven is smiling and angels are celebrating because God's will is being done on earth as it is in heaven.

INSIDE OUT

Read and reflect on the following verses throughout the week. How do you see the process of permeation at work in the verses listed below?
- 1 John 5:2-4
- 2 Corinthians 3:3
- Psalm 40:8
- Jeremiah 24:7, 32:39

What heavenly or eternal quality do you want to make a treasure worth investing in?

In what way have you experienced the principle of permeation—where what you practice you learn to love over time?

7. TAKE HEART!

"Love the LORD, all his faithful people!
The LORD preserves those who are true to him,
but the proud he pays back in full. Be strong
and take heart, all you who hope in the LORD."
(Psalm 31:23, 24)

Sometimes words and phrases lose their power as they become translated from one language to another. There is a phrase that recurs only a few times in the Bible that conveys a thought-provoking word picture. The phrase "take heart" means to "let your heart be encouraged" or "be bolstered from within". Looking deeper into the essence of the word, it has to do with radiating a warm confidence or being warm-hearted. In other words: "stoke the fire in your heart". As you read the stories below apply the deeper meaning of "take heart" to each situation.

Jesus Forgives and Heals a Paralyzed Man (Matthew 9:1-8)
The image of four friends bringing the paralytic to be healed by Jesus is endearing. The four stretcher-bearers tear through the roof to lower their friend at the feet of Jesus. The Scripture reads, "When Jesus saw their faith he said to the man, 'Take heart, son; your sins are forgiven'" (Matthew 9:1, 2).

Jesus Heals the Woman with the Issue of Blood (Matthew 9:20-22)
In this story it is clear that, with Jesus, no one is ever gets lost in the crowd. An unnamed woman suffering from an awful affliction touched the hem of his garment, not out of some superstitious reach, but out of a brazen hope in the grace of power of the God of Israel. Do you recall how God commanded the men to put tassels on the hem of their garments to remember God's revealed will and provision for the wayward Israelites (Numbers 15:34-37; Deuteronomy 22:12)? Jesus turned and saw her, saying, "'Take heart, daughter, your faith has healed you.' And the woman was healed at that moment" (Matthew 9:22).

Jesus Opens the Eyes of Blind Bartimaeus (Mark 10:46-52)
On His way to Jerusalem, Jesus encountered a blind man who calls out the Messianic name, "Son of David" in a manner that caused the disciples to attempt to suppress him. Read the whole story and you will see that

the man would not be quieted; instead Bartimaeus shouted even louder. Notice: "Jesus stopped and said, 'Call him.' So they called to the blind man, 'Cheer up! On your feet! He's calling you.' Throwing his cloak aside, he jumped to his feet and came to Jesus" (Mark 10:49, 50). The story ends with the blind man not only receiving sight, but also following Jesus.

Jesus Comforts His Disciples (John 16:16-33)
In the Gospel of John, Jesus informs the disciples about His eminent victory over sin and death and the coming of the Holy Spirit, saying, "I have told you these things, so that in me you may have peace. In this world you will have trouble. But take heart! I have overcome the world" (John 16:33). The book of John was written almost 60 years after Jesus's resurrection to combat the divergent claims many had about Christianity. The message to "take heart" would be even more meaningful to those believers who would soon be persecuted for their faith in Christ.

As you survey the above stories, consider how those who were told to "take heart" would be stirred to a deep conviction about who Jesus is.

INSIDE OUT

Which narrative do you resonate with? Why?

If Jesus were to meet you today and say, "Take heart," what area of your life do you think He would be encouraging you about?

8. DECLARE YOUR HEART!

*"I will utter hidden things, things from
of old—things we have heard and known,
things our ancestors have told us. We will not
hide them from their descendants; we will tell
the next generation the praiseworthy deeds of
the LORD, his power, and the wonders
he has done." (Psalm 78:2-4)*

When a crime is committed in full view of the public, you would think that it would be easy to have "witnesses" give "testimony" about what happened before their very eyes. Not so. In fact, more and more authorities are reporting increasing difficulty to get people to say what they saw. Some are even so bold as to declare, "I witnessed the crime, but I will not testify." The reasons are obvious: 1) Testifying makes you vulnerable, responsible, and accountable; 2) Testifying takes time and energy; and 3) Testifying is frightening because of the irreversible nature of the act. For many, the guilt of not speaking up becomes rationalized by a cynical view of justice and over time it becomes like a callous over the conscience. On the other hand, those who get involved in the process may experience stress and trepidation, but in the end, few actually regret their willingness to testify.

Court language is everywhere throughout the New Testament. Bearing "witness" on behalf of Christ is mentioned no less than twenty-five times. Giving testimony on behalf of Christ is mentioned well over a hundred times. The fundamental difference between people who "believe" and the people who are "convicted" may be best seen in their willingness to testify. Moreover, the experience of declaring what you know deepens the conviction in your own heart. In Psalm 78 you notice the songwriter's unwillingness to keep silent about the story of God and His people. You might also note the stark contrast between unwilling witnesses of crimes today and the indomitable witness of believers who relentlessly testify with conviction. Consider a few snapshots throughout scripture:

Jeremiah's Testimony
If you read all of Jeremiah 20, you will note that the prophet is chained

up in a stockade and tortured prior to declaring, "But if I say, 'I will not mention His word or speak anymore in His name,' His word is in my heart like a fire, a fire shut up in my bones. I am weary of holding it in; indeed, I cannot" (Jeremiah 20:9).

Peter and John
While Peter and the disciples refused to speak up about their loyalties when Jesus was arrested, in Acts 4:18, 19 there is no way they can remain silent: "Then they called them in again and commanded them not to speak or teach at all in the name of Jesus. But Peter and John replied, 'Which is right in God's eyes: to listen to you, or to him? You be the judges! As for us, we cannot help speaking about what we have seen and heard.'"

Shadrach, Meshach, and Abednego
Standing before Nebuchadnezzar the young followers of God were challenged to fall down and worship the image made to bear witness to the king as a deity. While the story of their faithful resistance is famous, note how their words are court-ready testimonies:

"Shadrach, Meshach and Abednego replied to him, 'King Nebuchadnezzar, we do not need to defend ourselves before you in this matter. If we are thrown into the blazing furnace, the God we serve is able to deliver us from it, and he will deliver us from Your Majesty's hand. But even if he does not, we want you to know, Your Majesty, that we will not serve your gods or worship the image of gold you have set up'" (Daniel 3:16-18).

There is no denying what happens when you bear witness, speak your heart, declare your loyalty, testify to what you know, and share your story. The heart grows with strength each time you speak up what you have witnessed. May your story tell the great things God has done in you today.

INSIDE OUT

Your testimony: read the following stories and consider how a testimony is simple and personal. In some cases it's a brief story about what God has done for you. In other examples it is simply a question or an incomplete declaration of the facts.
- Mark 5:1-20
- John 4:1-26, 28, 39-42; 9:1, 2

Throughout the week, read and reflect on what it looks like and sounds like to bear witness.

9. BE AWARE OF YOUR HEART

"Now my soul is troubled,
and what shall I say? 'Father, save me
from this hour'? No, it was for this
very reason that I came to this hour."
(John 12:27)

When you live by conviction, you sometimes have to do things you wouldn't otherwise choose. As you witness the Savior embrace the unimaginable task of dying for humanity, you will notice a few important checkpoints Jesus negotiates that may help you.

Checkpoint #1 "My soul is troubled…"
Name your feelings. Throughout His life Christ Jesus felt compassion, anger, zeal, and distress. There were moments when Jesus grieved in deep sorrow and others when He was full of joy. He felt love, amazement, and was, at times, deeply moved. The Son of God wept, groaned, sighed, and even felt indignant. What is critical is the fact that Jesus was able to identify and name His feelings. Sometimes people will use a generic word like "mad" or "sad" to convey their feelings when they really feel neglected, disrespected, underappreciated, or misunderstood. The key is to be specific about what you are feeling so you can know where it is coming from.

Jesus felt compassion; he was angry, indignant, and consumed with zeal; He was troubled, greatly distressed, very sorrowful, depressed, deeply moved, and grieved; He sighed; He wept and sobbed; He groaned; He was in agony; He was surprised and amazed; He rejoiced very greatly; He greatly desired, and He loved.

Checkpoint #2 "And what shall I say? 'Father rescue me from this hour.'"
Articulate the implications are. It is not enough to leave what might seem obvious unsaid. Jesus honestly admitted that His soul was "troubled". When you spell out the situation and say how each choice plays out to a certain conclusion, then you can make a better decision. Jesus comes right out says what would happen if He mindlessly obeyed His emotions—He would ask to be saved rather than go forward to save humanity. Sometimes all you need to do is spell out the implications and doing so makes the next step obvious.

Checkpoint #3 "Restate your goal."
Jesus came to do many things, but essentially one thing: "For the Son of man is come to seek and to save that which was lost" (Luke 19:10). "Even as the Son of man came not to be ministered unto, but to minister, and to give his life a ransom for many" (Matthew 20:28). "For I came down from heaven, not to do mine own will, but the will of him that sent me" (John 6:38). If there was one basic temptation leveled at Jesus, it was to take a different road than the one the Father had planned. The humanity of Jesus is unveiled as He identifies His emotions, logically plays out the situation, and ultimately states what the goal is—to give Himself to save humanity. How ironic it is to hear the religious leaders taunt Jesus with, "Save yourself, and come down from the cross" or imagine the criminals chiding, "If You are the Christ, save yourself and us!"

Given Jesus's example, what would this look like for you? As obstacles and challenges surround you, how do you respond? Even if the task before you is a decision between several good things, consider the checkpoints for conviction and put them to the test. Know that your emotions are as much a part of your brain as the part that computes mathematical equations. Knowing how to think through your situation enables you be true to what God has called you to. May the decisions you make be bathed in the wisdom of God's plan with trust in His ability to carry you home.

INSIDE OUT

Rarely does a voice from heaven speak in an audible and undeniable way. In the passage for today the voice of God is heard by the crowd, which suggests that this decision was in fact a defining moment in the ministry of Jesus. Why do you think the audible "voice of God" is not often heard anymore?

When in your life have you "heard God speak"? If not at all, then what is the closest that you have come to a moment of divine intervention?

As you surveyed some of the emotions of Jesus, which seem to amplify His humanity more than His divinity? Why do you think we tend to see some emotions as more "God-like" and some more human?

10. REVIVAL OF THE HEART

"Create in me a pure heart, O God, and renew a steadfast spirit within me. Do not cast me from your presence or take your Holy Spirit from me. Restore to me the joy of your salvation and grant me a willing spirit, to sustain me." (Psalm 51:10-12)

When this Psalm is sung, it is beautiful. When the passage is read, it rings with poetry. When you ruminate on this heartfelt prayer to God, it feels uplifting. When you consider that this was penned by a self-sufficient, womanizing murderer who was quick to demand the death penalty for someone who barbecued another man's sheep—well, it changes how you hear the song. However, let's not get too far ahead of the story.

First, consider the way of sheep. They are not considered the brightest of all creatures and they are predictable. Maybe you recall some of the parables or analogies in scripture that involve sheep getting lost. Sheep tend to be shortsighted, in that they often follow the greenest grass that is only inches from their noses. Little by little they often lead themselves far away from the herd. Sheep are not overtly rebellious per se, but simply get lost one subtle bite at a time… much like people.

It can be said of David that he knew sheep better than he knew himself. David is a case study of a man who ventured full speed to extremes, crashing headlong into success as well as failure. His heroic climb to the place of king is a storybook tale of the little guy making it big. The years when David ruled Israel are considered to be the golden era of great glory. Like the sheep David used to guide and protect, he got lost—very lost. You can read the details in 2 Samuel 11, but what matters is how David became so dull, calloused, and disconnected from his own convictions. Little by little, David nibbled himself out of the pasture and off into the wilderness. However, in his own mind King David did not see how lost he was. Because the king's heart was so callused, the prophet Nathan had to tell a parable and sneak up on David to wake him up.

Read the story for yourself:

"And the LORD sent Nathan to David. He came to him and said to him, 'There were two men in a certain city, the one rich and the other poor. The rich man had very many flocks and herds, but the poor man had nothing but one little ewe lamb, which he had bought. And he brought it up, and it grew up with him and with his children. It used to eat of his morsel and drink from his cup and lie in his arms, and it was like a daughter to him. Now there came a traveler to the rich man, and he was unwilling to take one of his own flock or herd to prepare for the guest who had come to him, but he took the poor man's lamb and prepared it for the man who had come to him.' Then David's anger was greatly kindled against the man, and he said to Nathan, 'As the LORD lives, the man who has done this deserves to die, and he shall restore the lamb fourfold, because he did this thing, and because he had no pity.'" (2 Samuel 12:1-6)

Have you ever had a friend or a loved one who was headed in the wrong direction, but couldn't see it? It is like someone being blind, yet going about his or her life as if having perfect vision; the person seems so far from the reach of God.

Even after the very carefully crafted parable, David still did not see himself as a wicked person. David was ready to dole out justice. At that point, Nathan was forced to tell David, "You are that man." Imagine the shock when the king realized what a horror he had become.

Now read the song again. Knowing what David did and now what he is asking God to do for him, does your heart cry out for a more severe justice or does it cry out a grateful praise to God for His grace? Because, according to the Bible—that sinner is you! "All have sinned and fallen short of the glory of God" (Romans 3:23). No one is exempt.

So sing David's song—because it's your song. Rejoice that...

God can bring deep conviction on the most stubborn heart.
God's mercy is always more effective than we expect.
God's love can compel a lovely song out of the darkest soul.

INSIDE OUT

Have you had moments in your life when conviction fell on you like a brick? Or was the revival a slow, steady awareness of your own brokenness? Take this week to write a Psalm penning the story of your redemption.

BEING HUMAN

Perhaps one of the perennial questions people have about people is, "Are humans essentially good or basically evil?" The word of God conveys that humans are made in the image of God, but also marred by the stain of sin. Humanity displays the capacity for inexplicable horror as well as unimaginable acts of love. You will notice in this section how the word of God unveils the majesty of good and the brutal honesty about what is evil. You will also come face to face with a choice to foster your sinful nature or the glory of God that is in you. Ultimately, there are so many unanswered questions about the nature of the world, God, and humans, but the unanswered questions do not relieve the need to cultivate your convictions about what you know.

11. ON BEING HUMAN

"For you created my inmost being; you knit me together in my mother's womb. I praise you because I am fearfully and wonderfully made... Your eyes saw my unformed body; all the days ordained for me were written in your book before one of them came to be."
(Psalm 139:14-16)

Gondwe wore glasses given to him as a young child because his vision was so poor he would have been classified "legally blind". For years he looked at the world with a little more clarity, but life was still mostly a blur. When an eye doctor came through the village with a box of donated glasses, Gondwe experimented with all of them. When he placed one pair on his face and looked through he jumped in surprise. He saw vivid details and complex features that were only a blur before. Again, his vision was not perfect, but he would say, "I see so clearly now."

Through what lens do you look at life? What is your worldview? When you compare all of the religions and "belief systems" of the world there seem to be about five basic questions that people are asking regarding life on earth:
1. Is there a God or a Prime Reality?
2. What is the meaning of life?
3. What is death?
4. What is the nature of ethics—right or wrong?
5. Finally—what does it mean to be human?

Since so much of what you think has to do with people, it is safe to say that everyone goes through life with an idea of what it means to be human. Whether you are aware of your assumptions or not, you see people through a lens—a worldview.

Maybe you have heard people say, "I believe people are essentially good." It seems a little hard to imagine that many would believe all of humanity is basically selfish or evil. What do you think? How would you explain or answer that question more fully?

When you consider what believers say about the nature of humanity, there is a collective cheer for being made unique, and good—even wonderful. In David's song above, he celebrates the handiwork of God in the make-up of people. How can he boast such things about humanity? God said so Himself. In the creation account where the Creator unveils the blueprint of His masterpiece the Bible says, "Then God said, 'Let us make mankind in our image, in our likeness'" (Genesis 1:26).

One conviction that should stir every believer is that human nature is rooted in the goodness of God. Paul echoes this truth, saying, "For he chose us in him before the creation of the world to be holy and blameless in his sight. In love he predestined us for adoption to sonship through Jesus Christ, in accordance with his pleasure and will…" (Ephesians 1:4,5). Keep reading Paul's statement and he includes the plan of redemption, forgiveness of sins, and the ultimate plan to restore humanity to glory. In other words, what God knew about the future controversy that would take place on earth did not change His plan to make people "in His image".

The question is: why? Maybe it is because His purpose for us is to be *with* Him. If we are in some ways *like* our Creator, then one of those qualities must be our need for community. According to Genesis 3, "God was walking in the garden in the cool of the day and asked, 'Where are you?'". After sin reared its ugly head in the hearts of humanity God announced, "Let them make me a sanctuary that I may dwell with them" (Exodus 25:8). All this was a sample of what would happen when the Creator or "the Word became flesh and dwelt among us. And we have seen His glory…" (John 1:14). Skip to the end of the story in Revelation 21:3 where the final goal of human purpose is achieved, and Jesus says, "Look! God's dwelling place is now among the people, and he will dwell *with* them."

Like a magnet, there is something in you that compels you, not only to be like God, but to be *with* God. May your view of you and God clarify and refine in such a way that you praise your Maker because you are "fearfully and wonderfully made".

INSIDE OUT

List the many qualities or characteristics of God that are unique to humans. List also the qualities of God that are unique to Him alone.

This week, practice specific characteristics that you want to cultivate in you that are like your Creator.

Pray each day and give specific thanksgiving for a part of you that you know was born in the creative mind of God.

12. CROSS-EYED

"Therefore, just as sin entered the world through one man, and death through sin, and in this way death came to all people, because all sinned…" (Romans 5:12)

It can also be said that, "Humans, at the very heart, are evil." As Paul explains in the key passage above, sin "came to all people" through the fall. Early in the history of the earth people became so corrupt that God resolved to destroy the earth and start over. Consider how the scriptures describe human nature at its worst: "The LORD saw how great the wickedness of the human race had become on the earth, and that every inclination of the thoughts of the human heart was only evil all the time" (Genesis 6:5). Notice all the superlatives: "*Every* inclination… was *only* evil *all* the time."

Sin has only one result—death. It would be nice to assume that if everyone could just think positively, live morally, and be friendly, the world would ultimately become a better place. It's a lie. Even good deeds can be done from a corrupt motivation. The first deception features the evil one lying to God's children, saying, "You will not certainly die" (Genesis 3:4). There is no vaccine or alternate method of rehabilitation—if you are human, you will die.

Praise God! One of the biggest words in the Bible is the three-letter word "but". Romans 6:23 states: "The wages of sin is death, but the gift of God is eternal life in Christ Jesus our Lord." God provided an answer to the problem, beginning with what He alone could do at the cross: "Consequently, just as one trespass resulted in condemnation for all people, so also one righteous act resulted in justification and life for all people. For just as through the disobedience of the one man the many were made sinners, so also through the obedience of the one man the many will be made righteous" (Romans 5:18, 19).

Have you ever thought about how unfair it is that you were born deserving death because of one person's disobedience? The scales of justice seem to tip back with the good news that one person's righteous life can pay for all. If you find that this is mind-boggling, you are not alone. Think about it.

Wrestle with it. Imagine it. Ultimately, you have to decide if you will accept the truth about who you are and what Jesus Christ has done to save you.

There are two realities to keep in mind as you personally live with conviction in your "human nature". First, you daily embrace the distance God crossed to win you. Secondly, you daily embrace another voice that checks your mind.

Cross Over
At the fall, when Adam and Eve first sinned, the result was death. Like a disease, everyone born from Eden's parents is corrupted with sin. Isaiah described the human condition well by saying, "Surely the arm of the LORD is not too short to save, nor his ear too dull to hear. But your iniquities have separated you from your God; your sins have hidden his face from you, so that he will not hear" (Isaiah 59:1, 2). Depend on grace to bridge the distance. Nothing else will cross the chasm between you and God—not education skill, talent, power or position, popularity or influence. It cannot even be crossed by doing great works in the world on behalf of humanity.

Cross-check
If you ever fly on an airplane, you will hear one attendant announce a pre-flight procedure called "cross-check" to the other attendants, which means that after you do your job someone else confirms it. The idea behind this precaution is not to distrust yourself, but to *not solely trust yourself*. When you consider the most reckless people in history, you may find that they solely trusted their own impulses. The wise man wrote in Proverbs 3:5, 6: "Trust in the LORD with all your heart and lean not on your own understanding; in all your ways submit to him, and he will make your paths straight." Granted, everyone has to use his or her own brain when discerning right from wrong. However, where the sinful human nature leads you to listen only to yourself, a healthy cross-check invites God's word to modify, rebuke, remind, reform, and re-direct your thoughts.

As you consider the voices that speak to you, from within and from without, may grace and wisdom keep you.

INSIDE OUT

Reflect on the strength of the voice of your nature that urges you to self-reliance. In what areas of your life do you tend to think you are in control or think you know yourself well?

Write or share with other believers and friends about your convictions concerning human nature and God's plan of salvation. What do you confidently believe? What do you still feel uncertain about?

13. TRAINING

*"Although I want to do good,
evil is right there with me. For in my inner
being I delight in God's law; but I see another
law at work in me, waging war against the
law of my mind and making me a prisoner of
the law of sin at work within me."
(Romans 7:21-23)*

Again, human nature is broken with sin, but also made in the image of God. Two impulses co-exist and compete in everyone born into the human race. Even though people are a long way from Eden, and the effects of sin are profound, the glory of God's character may still be displayed in humanity—in you.

Knowing that two natures battle within everyone, how does this change take place? Maybe you or someone you know has tried to overcome a habit or change into a more faithful follower of Christ, but always seem to lose the battle. First, know that you are not alone and this is a feeling every believer experiences.

Many are inquiring, "How am I to surrender myself to God?" You desire to give yourself to Him, but you are weak in moral power, in slavery to doubt, and controlled by the habits of your life of sin. Your promises and resolutions are like ropes of sand. You cannot control your thoughts, your impulses, or your affections. The knowledge of your broken promises and forfeited pledges weakens your confidence in your own sincerity, and causes you to feel that God cannot accept you; but you need not despair (STC p.47). Sometimes what keeps a person from embracing his or her human nature is the memory of failure. Even though part of you longs for God's grace and power to lead, there is a darkness, a weakness that also gets in the way of your faith. The following insight is pivotal:

"What you need to understand is the true force of the will. This is the governing power in the nature of man, the power of decision, or of *choice*. Everything depends on the right action of the will. The power of choice

God has given to men; it is theirs to *exercise*. You cannot change your heart, you cannot of yourself give to God its affections; but you can choose to serve Him. You can give Him your will; He will then work in you to will and to do according to His good pleasure. Thus your whole nature *will be* brought under the control of the Spirit of Christ; your affections will be centered upon Him, your thoughts will be in harmony with Him." (SC 47.1; emphasis added.) Consider three elements in the quotation above that are key to training for the battle of your nature.

Choice
You must decide, as many times as it takes, to follow God's revealed will for your life. Whether it is a choice between purity or self-indulgence, mercy or retaliation, honesty or duplicity, there is always a right choice to make.

Effort
Know that our effort is not what wins our eternal home—only the finished work of Christ on Calvary can pay your way home. However, your effort to practice a godly life is the way to cultivate God's image in you. Effort is not about trying to win salvation, but practicing virtue and righteousness in order to display God's glory. You will fail from time to time, but your Savior did not. You might fall in weakness, but Christ's victory for you is sure. You might stumble as you try to walk, but keep walking until you are home.

Time
In the same way that a well-worked muscle takes time to strengthen or a plant requires time to grow, the work of transformation occurs over time. Sometimes believers frustrate the work of grace by not trusting that God will achieve His glorious goal in the fullness of time. Simply look at everything that grows by God's creative hand and you will see how that good change takes time. That time period is a natural component of transformation.

So, it is time to train. May you discover the strength in your will and the peace of God's grace that empowers you to carry on.

INSIDE OUT

Read and reflect on the passages that will help you practice the three elements of cross training in the Christian life.

14. FROM SLAVE-ATION TO SALVATION

"My soul languishes for Your salvation;
I wait for your word." (Psalm 119:81)

The most common spelling mistake people make when typing the word "salvation" is to misspell it by typing "slavation". While it doesn't show on the printed page, word processing software will have the word underlined in red. The auto-correct on computers changes the spelling for you, but the connection between slavery and salvation is not a mistake. *Salvation*. The word is used over a hundred times in the Bible and it basically means "to deliver out of", which is why the Exodus from Egypt and the long trek to the Promised Land are the perfect illustration of what God does for you today.

Where did this hunger and quest for salvation begin? Is it simply Plan B if Adam and Eve chose to disobey and thereby fall? If you believe what Paul said in Ephesians 1:3-14, then the story started before the creation of the world, when God started thinking about people. The question that the teacher of the law earnestly inquired is at the center of the human deepest human need: "What must I do to inherit eternal life?" (Luke 10:25-37; Mark 10:17-31). Humanity longs for more than the absence of oppression or freedom from guilt, it cries out for a reward, an eternal home (2 Peter 3:13).

The experience of salvation slowly steeped in Nicodemus and Joseph of Arimathea, who were considered "secret believers" that ultimately became full-on disciples after Christ had been crucified (John 3; 7:50; 9:39; 19:38). The Samaritan woman, suspiciously stirred by the conversation with Christ, left her water jar to share with the whole town a compelling testimony in one simple question, "Could this be the Christ?" (John 4:4-42). Don't forget that Jesus granted and assured the death-bed-request of the thief on the cross (Luke 23:35-43). Today, the same assurance is given to all who believe and receive (John 1:10-12) and those who by faith ask for the gift of eternal life. Each one made the leap of faith to let God deliver them.

Lifeguards are often taught not to try to save someone who is thrashing and flailing in the water. It is safer to wait until people are not trying to save themselves to then bring them to safety. It's also not easy to let someone save you. The urge to try to help your savior only complicates the saving process. Lifeguards are typically strong and skilled enough to swim you back to safety—if you let them.

If there is a plea from God in the pages of scripture it is this: it's safe to let God rescue you. It's safe to believe. It's safe to rest in His finished work of salvation. It's safe, but it may not be easy. Review the following passages and note how the key word that is italicized highlights different parts of the experience of salvation.

"Then I heard a loud voice in heaven say: '*Now* have come the salvation and the power and the kingdom of our God, and the authority of his Messiah.'" (Revelation 12:10)

"Though you have not seen him, you love him; and even though you do not see him now, you believe in him and are filled with an inexpressible and glorious joy, for *you are receiving* the end result of your faith, the salvation of your souls." (1 Peter 1:9)

"For I am not ashamed of the gospel, because it is the *power* of God that brings salvation to everyone who believes: first to the Jew, then to the Gentile." (Romans 1:16)

"Salvation is found in no one else, for there is *no other name* under heaven given to mankind by which we must be saved." (Acts 4:12)

"With joy *you will draw* water from the wells of salvation." (Isaiah 12:3)

May your heart-longing for safety, deliverance, and restoration be something you experience today.

INSIDE OUT

Which words capture the experience of salvation for you? If you had to choose only three words, which three would you choose? Why?

Word/Story Association
In a group or on your own, scan through the words and when you think of a particular word, which story in the Bible comes to your mind first?

Think about your friends/associates who may not know the Savior. What words do you think would resonate with them? Which terms do you think would be foreign or an obstacle to their understanding of the gospel?

UNDER CONVICTION

Nothing stirs the soul like seeing someone on fire with conviction. To know, believe, embrace a truth so much so that you are willing risk life and limb to live according to your heart—that is inspiring. In this section look, listen, and learn from lives of people under conviction. Some are famous and others are nameless mentions in the biblical story. The storied lives of the following people capture some of the more pressing attributes of the quest for conviction.

15. NOT SO DEAD END

"I am the resurrection and the life.
The one who believes in me will live, even
though they die; and whoever lives by
believing in me will never die."
(John 11:25, 26)

Questions are the power tools of communication. Sometimes questions convey an idea rather than collect information. Lawyers question witnesses; doctors question patients; children question teachers; parents are always asking questions of teenagers while teenagers question everything about anything. Some questions are silly: "Do you want to go to bed without dinner?" or "How would you feel if I stepped on your toe?" When you don't have all the information, you ask a question. When you want someone to respond, take action, feel an emotion, or simply offer insight, you ask. People have questions they ask of God. Why did this happen to me? Where is God when bad things happen?

More important than any question you might have for God are the questions He has for you. One of the most telling questions Jesus asked came to Martha at the death of her brother Lazarus, where Jesus declared, "I am the resurrection and the life. The one who believes in me will live, even though they die..." (John 11:23-26). If this is true, then everything about life changes—everything.

What humanity fears, but can't escape, is the reality of death. It's strange how the one thing everyone on the planet ultimately experiences, save Enoch and Elijah, is met with protest. The impulse is so basic, yet so profound. You are not meant to die, but to live. And although everyone should face death with a certain attitude of acceptance, most people approach the end with defiance. Again, could this be God's image in you recoiling against something you were never meant for?

If what Jesus is saying is true, then His follow-up question is critical: "Do you believe this?" This is not a rhetorical question. There is no intent to convey a truth beyond what is already spoken. The Savior is asking for a response: "Do you believe this?" What is your answer?

The majority of people who live on this planet long to go to a better place. The Australian Aborigines pictured heaven as a distant island just beyond the western horizon. The early Finns thought heaven was a glorious island that loomed in the far away east. Mexicans, Peruvians, and Polynesians believed that they went to the sun or the moon after death. Native Americans held that, in the afterlife, their spirits would hunt the spirits of buffalo. The ancient Babylonian Gilgamesh epic describes a resting place of heroes and hints at a tree of life. In the pyramids of Egypt, those embalmed for their season of rest had maps placed beside them to guide their journey to the future world. The Romans assured themselves that those who were good would picnic in the Elysian Fields, while their horses grazed in green meadows.

The whole story from scripture displays it. Jesus promises it. Movies depict it. Advertisers use it. The grand narrative of God and people ends and renews. The question remains: do you live with the conviction that death is a stop, but not the end? If that conviction resides in you, the apostle Paul would say it is because of "who" is in you:

"But we have this treasure in jars of clay to show that this all-surpassing power is from God and not from us... We always carry around in our body the death of Jesus, so that the life of Jesus may also be revealed in our body. For we who are alive are always being given over to death for Jesus's sake, so that his life may also be revealed in our mortal body. So then, death is at work in us, but life is at work in you" (2 Corinthians 4:7-12).

Why do you want to live and not die?

INSIDE OUT

Listed are several passages about the promise of life and the threat of death. Throughout the week, take time to declare your answer to the question Jesus asks Martha.
- Romans 8
- 1 Thessalonians 4:13-18
- 1 Corinthians 15:54, 55; 6:14
- Psalm 146:3, 4

If both death and life are within you, what specific things will you do this week to protest death and celebrate life?

Find a quiet place to pray aloud and answer God's question to Martha as if it is being spoken to you. Declare your understanding of His power over death and acknowledge the risen Christ living in you.

16. HOUSE RULES

"On reaching Jerusalem, Jesus entered the temple courts and began driving out those who were buying and selling there... he said, 'Is it not written: "My house will be called a house of prayer for all nations"? But you have made it a den of robbers.'"
(Mark 11:15-17)

If you had to express three of your deepest convictions, what would they be? This week's devotion examines the first of three moments when Jesus displayed unmistakable conviction. What did Jesus see in the temple courts that moved Him so deeply?

During Passover, there might have been over two million people in the Jerusalem area; the temple would have been packed with worshippers, travelers, and people facilitating the religious activities. Some would come to pay the temple tax, which was about two days' wages and was paid during the Passover. According to the gospel of Mark, people were using the courtyard to "carry merchandise through", indicating the place of worship had become a lucrative toll way. Most of all, there were added divisions to the temple courtyard, created by barriers.

The first barrier was the court of the Gentiles, the only place foreigners could stand and past which they were not allowed to go. Then there was the court of women; beyond this fence no woman was allowed to go. The next division was the court of the Israelites, where the men handed offerings to the priests and past which they could not go. Finally, there was the court of Priests, where only priests were permitted to enter and fulfill their duties at the altar of burnt offerings.

Over time, the temple and its system of barriers had become a bustling marketplace for economic gains. Do you remember why the temple was made in the first place? In Exodus 25:1 God said, "Have them make a sanctuary for me, and I will dwell among them." The purpose of the temple was to offer a place for communion—God being present with *all* people.

Jews and non-Jews came from all over the world for Passover. Foreigners who heard the stories of Jehovah came hungry and hopeful to find God. The world at that time had no prominent religion. Earnest seekers, like the Greeks, Simon of Cyrene and Ethiopian eunuch, travelled to meet the God of Israel face to face. Instead, worshippers and seekers found a market and a mob, and that moved Jesus to move the furniture around.

Jesus arrived at the temple and started cleaning as though it were His house! Note the conviction of Christ: anything that hinders ordinary people in their search for God should be relentlessly removed. His house, His rules. Over four hundred years earlier, God had spoken through Isaiah the prophet: Isaiah wrote a message from God about His temple.

"'Suppose outsiders want to follow me and serve me? They want to love me and worship me. They keep the Sabbath day and do not misuse it. And they are faithful in keeping my covenant. Then I will bring them to my holy mountain of Zion. I will give them joy in my house. They can pray there. I will accept their burnt offerings and sacrifices on my altar. My house will be called a house where people from all nations can pray.' The Lord and King will gather those who were taken away from their homes in Israel. He announces, 'I will gather them to myself. And I will gather others to join them.'" (Isaiah 56:6-8, NIrV)

Listen carefully to the heart of God yearn for the outsider. See how the temple was meant for anyone to approach? Now consider another thought: "Don't you know that you yourselves are God's temple and that God's Spirit dwells in your midst?" (1 Corinthians 3:16).

What now, if *you are the place where God is revealed* to the nations?

INSIDE OUT

What tables need to be turned over in your life? What barriers keep you and God from experiencing face-to-face communion? Have you assembled fences that facilitate your will instead of God's will in your life? Are there some people whom you think don't deserve to be near God?

Reflect on these passage this week. While this verse is in the context of avoiding sexual immorality, consider the principle this verse is grounded in, and the various areas of your life it can be applied.
- 1 Corinthians 6:19, 20
- Ephesians 2:19-22
- 1 Peter 2:5

17. FREE IN DEED

*"When Jesus saw her, he called her
forward and said to her, 'Woman, you are
set free from your infirmity.' Then he put
his hands on her, and immediately she
straightened up and praised God."*
(Luke 13:12, 13)

When in your life has someone's goodness granted you a feeling of freedom? Maybe it was a ride, a meal or a gift of food, or even someone stepping in and giving you much needed help with an overwhelming task. Whatever the gift, it likely gave you a sense that a weight was lifted off your back.

For believers in Jesus's day, next to breathing, eating and sleeping, there was nothing more routine than going to the synagogue on Sabbath. Sometimes routines can become a rut. Have you noticed how water automatically seeks a path of least resistance? A groove becomes a rut, becoming a channel, which then turns into a ditch that ultimately results in a canyon. In the depths of a canyon all you see is the sheer face of exposed rock and roots against the backdrop of a vast wall of dirt—the sidewalls of the canyon. High above may be a scene so glorious, but you will never see it until you climb up and out.

The more you repeat a thought or action, the more momentum that habit gains. In this week's story, the synagogue leader cultivated a habit of the mind about Sabbath. For eighteen years a crippled woman found her way to synagogue every Sabbath. Every week she labored over the cobblestone streets noting how each rock looked like the other. However, on this particular day Jesus "saw" her and placed his healing hand on her back, instantly healing her. How could anyone witness this miracle and not be moved with awe and wonder?

The local "spiritual leader" had dug himself into a rut so deep that he had forgotten synagogues were established to be places to pass on the knowledge of God. When the temple was destroyed, the Jews established synagogues to be places of learning, practice, and faith-building experiences for the children of God. After the synagogue leader made his point about proper Sabbath-keeping, the Savior unloaded the full force of His heart, saying, "You hypocrites! Doesn't each of you on the Sabbath untie your ox or donkey from the stall and lead it out to give it water? Then should not this woman, a daughter of Abraham, whom Satan has kept bound for eighteen long years, be set free on the Sabbath day from what bound her?" (Luke 13:15).

Consider this paraphrase: "You blind pretenders! Fakers! How can you witness this miracle with your own eyes but be so blinded by your habit of thought? Because you are in the ditch you only see the dirt and not a display of grace! You could have rediscovered the Exodus! Instead, you are so near-sighted you don't even realize that you treat your donkey better than a daughter of Abraham—your sister in God! If you knew the real significance of Sabbath you would shout, 'You are free! You are free! We are all free indeed!'" The apostles, seized by the conviction of Christ, joined the freedom chorus boldly: "It is for freedom that Christ has set us free. Stand firm, then, and do not let yourselves be burdened again by a yoke of slavery" (Galatians 5:1).

Will your Sabbath be a celebration where people are set free? Even if you spent all Sabbath bearing witness and celebrating how God liberates people, you would be renewed. May the same hand that touched weary backs long ago make you free today.

INSIDE OUT

Practices and habits are developed through repetition and time. Notice how Jesus patterned His ministry with prayer.

Mark 1:35; Luke 4:42; Luke 6:12; Mark 6:46; Luke 5:16

What habits would you like to cultivate? Below are passages that describe the nature and work of habit formation. Examine what the Bible says and choose a new endeavor you want to turn into a practice.
- Hebrews 5:14
- Luke 4:16
- Acts 2:46, 17:2
- Judges 2:19
- Hebrews 10:25
- 1 Timothy 5:13
- Jeremiah 13:23

18. SOLVING THE PROBLEM

"Jesus went through all the towns and villages, teaching in their synagogues, proclaiming the good news of the kingdom and healing every disease and sickness. When he saw the crowds, he had compassion on them, because they were harassed and helpless, like sheep without a shepherd."
(Matthew 9:35-37)

Problems. In every family or friend group there are at least three types of problem solvers: fixers, those who figure it out as you go, and those who become aware of the problem after a solution is found. Imagine how the disciples measured the problem of so many people, with so many different needs, with only one place to bring their pain—Jesus. What would stir up a whirlwind of consternation in a committee meeting moved the Son of God with compassion. When in your life have you faced trouble popping around you all at once, like corn kernels popping on a hot griddle?

The Gospel of Matthew portrays people coming to Jesus in crowds. Jesus was not surprised by the problem, for He knew the world He lived in. His compassion is not for the pain as much as it is for something even more troubling—the people evidently had nowhere to go. The Lord describes the real issue saying, "They are harassed and helpless, like sheep without a shepherd." Everyone is exposed to pain and suffering, but if there is hope, the misery is only temporary. However, when relief does not even seem possible, hurt becomes agony and any heartache erupts into despair.

Compassion. The word is only used of Jesus and you will be hard-pressed to find a stronger term for a human emotion. "Compassion" is a medical reference to the intestines twisting and crying out. In the New Testament world, the center of the human being housed the seat of human emotions, therefore, when Jesus is "moved" with compassion, it's more than pity, more than sympathy, and more than empathy. When Jesus saw the crowds, *He doubled over in pain and had to fix the problem.*

Solutions. If you could solve one problem today, which do you think would make the biggest difference in the world? Why?

- Food for the hungry
- Freedom from oppression
- Healing from disease
- Education for the ignorant
- Companionship for the lonely

Many seek to solve the problems of the world using strategies of human ingenuity. However, unless you recognize that the source of the problem is sin, then every attempt to fix the world and make it a better place will fail. Jesus came to answer the problem of sin, not to change the immediate situation. Even so, if you scan through the storied life of Christ, you will notice that every time the word "compassion" is used of Jesus, the Son of God is compelled to meet the aching need. A nameless widow on the road to bury her only son awakens compassion and Jesus speaks life to the dead. A leper asks for an end to his misery and another chance at life, and Jesus can't help but to heal him. And when the crowds bring their full range of trouble to Christ, He responds. But there is more. Like a good doctor or a skilled mechanic, Jesus diagnosed the problem and offers a solution: "The harvest is plentiful but the workers are few. Ask the Lord of the harvest, therefore, to send out workers into his harvest field" (Matthew 9:38).

Maybe you were expecting something more elaborate, but think about the genius of Christ's plan. If the heart of the Risen Christ abides in people through the work of the Holy Spirit, then the heart of God is multiplied in the world. According to Jesus, what the world needs now is more people who will respond with compassion to the pain in the world. The answer is more people. More workers. Jesus called for more people who would become one with lonely humanity. More people who would look long enough at their struggle and act. One could argue that the idea of church is one of Christ's deepest convictions.

INSIDE OUT

In the time of Jesus, the people longed for the hope of the Messiah, but nothing seemed to happen according to plan. Religious leaders offered a religion that was lifeless and the faithful began to question their faith. Reflect on your world today and compare the problems of the past to those of right now. How does Jesus's solution for issues back then relate to the problems people face today?

The task this week is to deliberately be the help that the harassed and helpless need.

19. THREE BELIEVERS, TWO IFS

"'…who is the god who will deliver you out of my hands?' Shadrach, Meshach, and Abednego answered and said to the king, '…our God whom we serve is able to deliver us from the burning fiery furnace, and he will deliver us out of your hand, O king.'"
(Daniel 3:15-18)

Has it ever occurred to you that little words like *if, and,* and *but* are just as crucial to Christianity as *propitiation, justification* or *predestination*? Some of the best stories, truest truths, and encouraging promises hinge on the little words of the Bible. In naming people of conviction, it would be a crime to pass over the three Hebrews living in Babylon. Nebuchadnezzar builds a statue and commands everyone to bow down and worship or be thrown into a fiery furnace. If you know the story, you know the boys choose not to bow down; instead they present the king with two "ifs" that shock the world.

If #1: *"If we are thrown into the furnace… God is able. And he will…"*
Most believers could declare the first "if"—that God *could* intervene. The first part of their answer bespeaks a basic belief: *God can.* In a similar way you might say…

"If cancer strikes… God can heal."
"If the car crashes… God can protect."
"If you are out of money… God can provide."
"If evil surrounds you… God can deliver."

But *will* He? While God is certainly always able, He does not always intervene. When He doesn't, we may not utterly forsake God, but the disappointment certainly can affect our view of God. Expecting God to intervene is a double-edged sword because if God *can* do something, we assume that He *should*, and therefore *will.*

If #2: *The second "if" catapults these three boys from ordinary to extraordinary.*
"But even *if* he does not, we want you to know, Your Majesty, that we will

not serve your gods or worship the image of gold you have set up." Between the first *if* and the second there is a space that often goes unnoticed. The space between "if God saves us from the fire" and "if God does not save us from the fire" may not seem like much on paper, but in life becomes a Grand Canyon separating immature faith from mature faith. To journey from one *if* to the next is the walk of Christian maturity. Immature faith tends to sing only the songs that are in range, play the notes that are effortless, preach the sermons that make you feel comfortable, and teach only the things you are sure of.

Three boys make it clear that they believe these three things. *"It's not about me."* There is a truth about God more important and more profound than my safety or my life. *"It's not a problem."* While I am unable to fix this problem, I am a child of the God who invented life with His lips and solves death with a plan. He can freeze your furnace or melt your statue to mud. If He chooses not to, He has promised to remake me in the twinkling of an eye with as little as a whisper. *"It's going to be ok."* The here and now is very scary, but the value of faithfulness to God is eternal and worth more than protecting my life in the moment that I face death.

You may not face literal "do or die" moments like these three Hebrews did long ago, but examine where your faith rests on the spectrum between "God can" and "even if God does not".

INSIDE OUT

If faith in God is like a muscle, how does faith strengthen and mature? Five exercises to try this week:
- Seize pivotal moments—take a stand or a step back, but make use of the moments you are given.
- Trust the process over time—growth happens like the dawn and sunset, not the flipping of a light switch.
- Practice an active trust—take a leap of faith in the words you speak or the deeds you do for others.
- Live principled lives—reflect and name the principles you will not compromise.
- Seek to collaborate—you were not meant to grow alone, but in community with other believers who encourage one another.

20. A DIFFERENT KIND OF KING

"Be strong and courageous.
Do not be afraid or discouraged because
of the king of Assyria and the vast army with
him, for there is a greater power with us than
with him. With him is only the arm of flesh,
but with us is the LORD our God to help
us and to fight our battles."
(2 Chronicles 32:6, 7)

Read again the words Hezekiah spoke above and reflect for a moment on the kind of person that might say such a thing. Who do you know that is an immovable rock of conviction? It doesn't mean the person is inflexible or irrationally stubborn, but is someone who is reliable when it comes to the things that matter. There are people who live under conviction by remaining quiet and unobtrusive, and then there are people whose conviction causes them to lead brazenly. Hezekiah is somehow a combination of both. Hezekiah's life is filled with pivotal choices drawn from the deep well of conviction. "Hezekiah trusted in the LORD, the God of Israel. There was no one like him among all the kings of Judah, either before him or after him" (2 Kings 18:5).

His first project centered on restoring the work of the temple and later Hezekiah recaptured lost territories to the Philistines. This resolute leader refused to acknowledge Assyria's reign and even found ways to advance and engineer pools and water tunnels into the city (2 Kings 2:20).

At one point Hezekiah became sick; he sent for the prophet Isaiah, who surveyed the king's state and announced, "This is what the LORD says: Put your house in order, because you are going to die; you will not recover" (2 Kings 20:1). The prophet's words sank into the heart of the king and he cried. Like most people who learn of their imminent death, there is a protest. Some argue simply because they don't want their lives to end, but others long to see what their lives could still do. In the same way conviction is displayed in deeds, it is also conveyed in the prayers people pray. Hezekiah prayed, "'Remember, LORD, how I have walked before you faithfully and with wholehearted devotion and have done what is good in your eyes.' And Hezekiah wept bitterly" (2 Kings 20:3). This is either the prayer of someone arrogant and disillusioned, or the honest heart of a man who really is who he says he is.

If this were a movie or a play, the crowd would beg for a miracle. You would probably want good to come to this man just based on the fact that he's a decent guy. However, what you know about Hezekiah compels you to want not just a miracle for him; you also want a miracle to occur in the endeavor he has fought so hard for. Knowing that these stories don't always take the turn you want them to, be assured that it is safe to read the rest:

"Before Isaiah had left the middle court, the word of the LORD came to him: 'Go back and tell Hezekiah, the ruler of my people, "This is what the LORD, the God of your father David, says: 'I have heard your prayer and seen your tears; I will heal you. On the third day from now you will go up to the temple of the LORD. I will add fifteen years to your life. And I will deliver you and this city from the hand of the king of Assyria. I will defend this city for my sake and for the sake of my servant David.'"' (2 Kings 20:4-6)

If you ever wonder whether a person can move God to action because of who they are, wonder no more. While David is robed with the "man after God's own heart" moniker, Hezekiah rests peacefully in the same camp. As you look at this noble king's life, what are some qualities you feel compelled to embrace? As you live in faithfulness to God this week, practice your deepest convictions with grace and a steadfast heart.

INSIDE OUT

What do you think it means to "walk with God" with "whole-hearted devotion"? Who do you know that comes the closest to being described this way? Take time this week to send them a note or a message conveying what their faithfulness means to you.

Read and reflect on the following passages that display a challenge to the whole heart.
- 1 Samuel 12:20-25
- Jeremiah 29:13
- Psalm 138:1
- Acts 11:23

This week, consider praying for people in your life that you have influence with. Pray for your heart to be true and your witness to be effective.

21. FROM GOD TO GOD

"To the nations and peoples of every language, who live in all the earth: May you prosper greatly! It is my pleasure to tell you about the miraculous signs and wonders that the Most High God has performed for me. How great are his signs, how mighty his wonders! His kingdom is an eternal kingdom; his dominion endures from generation to generation."
(Daniel 4:1-3)

Whether real life story or fictional fairy tale, humanity cheers when the evil dictator goes down and the underdog wins. It is hard to imagine a culture where leaders can be perceived as gods. When you think about it, the first sin was the aspiration to become "like the Most High" (Isaiah 14:12-14). When rulers like Pharaoh, Nebuchadnezzar and Nero can issue a command that is obeyed without question, they begin to think they are not like everyone else. Only part of this mindset is accurate. In one sense, they are not like everyone else in that very few people in this world can say, "I want a salad, now!" and it appears in a matter of moments because servants are waiting to meet every request. While their temporal whims are granted, eventually they are forced to face their own mortality.

Pharaoh believed his authority was invincible, yet the plagues God sent overwhelmed him. While you eat the best food, possess the best doctors, and are protected against danger by a mighty army, you are still vulnerable—even fragile. Nero believed in his head that he was a god. The Roman emperor also suffered extreme paranoia, which is a syndrome of fear. How does a powerful god tremble with fear? No matter what heights you rise to, you are not God. Just thinking about elevating your station overestimates your humanity and underestimates divinity. In other words, whether you picture yourself as god or God, your standard for both shifts and the result is deception.

You might be tempted to think this is only possible with the rich and the powerful, but a god complex is something everyone born of Adam and Eve is prone to. Anytime you elevate yourself and lower God, you tread dangerously on the slippery slope of idolatry. Nebuchadnezzar's view of God changed in a moment. In Daniel 3, the world leader's belief about God swings from, "And who is the god who will deliver you out of my hands?" to "There is no other god who is able to rescue in this way" (Daniel 3:15, 29). The bigger you are, the larger the learning curve from self-worship to acknowledging Someone greater.

One principle that seems to run throughout scripture is that the miraculous may arrest your attention, but belief is a byproduct of faith in action. The Israelites who left Egyptian slavery witnessed unparalleled evidence of God's power and provision, yet they still "disbelieved" and ultimately ran to hand-made gods for help. Some think about the miracles Jesus performed and wish they could have seen leprosy cleansed and blind eyes opened. Maybe, if you could just see the miraculous, you would believe more. As much as you may want the invisible hand of God to show you a miracle, the reality is that when the smoke clears, the dust settles and the crowd disperses, even those who witness miracles can still experience doubt. It is possible they can ultimately disbelieve. Whether you see the miraculous or not, you still need to respond with a decision, a commitment or an action in order to cultivate belief.

Of course this is not true for everyone, but it would seem like the masses who experience the miraculous also fail to believe. When Jesus was arrested, where were the crowds who wanted to crown Him king when He filled their stomachs? When Jesus was on trial, who showed up to testify on behalf of their new vision, good hearing, or restored limbs? Nebuchadnezzar is not exempt from seeing and disbelieving. However, his legacy of faith is recorded in Daniel 4 and the testimony of this mighty king is eternally remarkable. Take a moment to read the whole story, then begin this week by checking your view of God and your view of yourself.

INSIDE OUT

In your mind, what are the best stories of the rise and fall of human ambition? What are some of the most profound stories of people who were exalted as a result of their humility?

Read and reflect on the following passages this week. Give special attention to the advice from Peter.
- 1 Peter 5:6
- Exodus 10:3
- Matthew 23:12
- James 4:10

22. TIMES TO PRAY

*"When Daniel knew that the document
had been signed, he went to his house where
he had windows in his upper chamber open
toward Jerusalem. He got down on his knees
three times a day and prayed and gave thanks
before his God, as he had done previously."
(Daniel 6:10)*

Was it because Daniel already had such deep conviction that he
did not hesitate to pray in the face of danger, or did praying
faithfully cause his core beliefs to run deeper than ever before? There are
courageous acts that are done in the heat of the moment, when crisis calls
for bravery. Rightly so, impulsive bravery is often awarded the badge of
"heroism". Even though it's less dramatic, how noble is the relentless faith
of one who pursues the path in the face of possible death?

One of the more renowned "one-liners" in the Bible is Jeremiah's
prophecy, where God promises, "'For I know the plans I have for you,'
declares the LORD, 'plans to prosper you and not to harm you, plans
to give you hope and a future'" (Jeremiah 29:11). What a beautiful
message for young people embarking on the cusp of life's great
adventure! However, that promise is couched in the context of another
more technical reality: "This is what the LORD says: 'When seventy
years are completed for Babylon, I will come to you and fulfill my good
promise to bring you back to this place'" (Jeremiah 29:10). The promise
of prosperity comes after seventy years of captivity—again. Daniel
knew that his life would be consumed in Babylon, but still he turned
his face to Jerusalem, remembering the promise, and praying gratefully
to His God.

Praying Purposefully
Praying toward Jerusalem not only symbolized God's purpose for His
people, but it postured Daniel in the direction of the temple. The temple
had been ransacked according to Daniel 5, and it is difficult to separate
the people of God from the sanctuary. If God was not currently dwelling in

the Most Holy Place, it is where God promised to meet His people. Daniel prayed toward the Holy Land on purpose.

Praying Gratefully
In prayer, Daniel "gave thanks". When you think about all Daniel could have been complaining about at that moment, it is astonishing to imagine anyone praising God with gratitude. What do you think Daniel would have been grateful for? There is a saying, *gratitude is mostly attitude*, and if this is true, then it makes sense why Daniel stands like a solid oak tree in a windstorm of uncertainty. Think about how you pray and how it might realign your attitude to pray more with thanksgiving.

Praying Consistently
Three times a day Daniel turned his faced to God and prayed. Some think the repetition has to do with meals, but it had very little to do with eating. The times for common prayer were 9:00 a.m., 12:00 noon, and 3:00 p.m. If you trace rebellion, apostasy, and apathy to a source, it may be a lack of awareness of God. Nothing makes you more aware of God's presence than anchoring the day in seasons of prayer. This practice is inconvenient and for many, unrealistic. Others dismiss the form because they equate the consistency with mindless religiosity, but have you tried praying according to a plan?

Praying Historically
The key phrase summing up Daniel's lifestyle of conviction is that he prayed "as he had done previously." Whether Daniel prayed because he was faithful or was faithful because he prayed is lost in the history of his unwavering devotion over time. Time has a way of refining our wants and whims to what we really desire.

This week, take the opportunity to practice a lifestyle of praying. As you pray, may the glory of God's promises shine on you and may the mouths of the lions in your life be shut.

INSIDE OUT

Read and reflect on the significance of organizing your prayer time. Some think it is helpful to pray when it is convenient, but instead set times to pray when it is best. Below are some passages for a frame of reference, but the key task is to practice praying prayers to God rich in gratitude and thanksgiving. See what happens.
- Matthew 6
- Acts 3, 4:23-30; 10:9
- Psalm 55:16, 17
- Daniel 9:21

23. GROWING CONVICTION

"'Everything is possible for one who believes.' Immediately the boy's father exclaimed, 'I do believe; help me overcome my unbelief!'"
(Mark 9:23, 24)

A "mountaintop experience" is that moment when you suddenly find yourself able to believe, see, or remember a truth not apparent in the ordinary circumstances of your reality. The problem with the mountaintop is that people live most of their lives in the valley. Then they wonder, "Why can't I just stay on the mountain?" Maybe it's because "easy faith" is an oxymoron. Faith is committing to what you can't see because of something you hope is true (Hebrews 11:1).

After a mountaintop experience, Jesus leaves to go down to the valley below. As Jesus leads His disciples down the mountain, they happen upon a diverse crowd of "believers". In this crowd there are full-on disciples of Christ, teachers of the law who don't want to believe, and people who are only there to see what is going on. Finally, there is a father bringing his son to Jesus.

The father encounters the disciples first; Peter, James, and John fail to liberate the boy. The crowd wonders. The teachers of the law mock the disciples, throwing sarcastic remarks about the ineptitude of Jesus's pupils. When Jesus encountered the crowd, He rebuked those who didn't want to believe, saying, "You unbelieving generation, how long shall I stay with you? How long shall I put up with you?" (Mark 9:19). Who do you think He was talking to?

Notice the beginning of the story: the father sought to "bring his son to Jesus" and after the arguing, Jesus tells the father, "Bring the boy to me." Some may posit that the cry of the father's heart when he blurts out, "But if you can do anything, take pity on us and help us" is nothing more than doubt—the kind of doubt that wrecks faith. However, notice a couple of beautiful facts about this father's apparent doubt. First of all, the "*if*" is actually part of faith's request. You could call it a "weak faith", "small faith", "incomplete faith", or "no faith", but you would be wrong. Everyone who believes must ask and this father simply asks for Jesus to heal his son, *if* He can. Would he have tried to get his son to Jesus or have even asked at all without a basic faith? Could he?

Secondly, the father asks for Jesus to "take pity on us and help us". *Us.* The father is so fully invested in the son's brokenness he can't see where the problem begins and ends. It is not his son's affliction alone—it belongs to both of them. So whose faith was more mature? The three Hebrews who were willing to die or a man who continues to leap off ledges for his son's healing, only to face one disappointment after another? Whose faith was greater—three paragons of faith who front up to the king at the opening of a fiery furnace or a father who stands in the middle of a mindless, bickering crowd willing himself to try anything to get help for his ailing son?

When Jesus responds by saying, "Anything is possible for one who believes," the father replies, "I do believe; help my unbelief." In other words, "I came to you. I brought him here. I showed up. I pray. I commit. I endure failure. I get my hopes up. I expect something good to happen, even when healing has never happened for my son. But I can't make myself believe more. I can't conjure up more faith. I believe, and although I hope against my doubts, I commit. I step off the edge and fall. So, this time, please catch me and my son." Where did we ever get the idea that doubt equals a lack of belief? They are related, but not the same.

So Jesus speaks. And the spirit leaves and it appears like the boy is dead. "The boy looked so much like a corpse that many said, 'He's dead.'" What if the story had ended there? Fortunately, the story ends with: "Jesus took him by the hand and lifted him to his feet, and he stood up." It goes to show that each time we trust Him in spite of uncertainty and doubt, our belief in His faithfulness is strengthened. And over time, even though there will always be ebbs and flows of faith in your life, if you don't let go of your beliefs, they will grow up into your commitments.

INSIDE OUT

Who do you relate to most in this story? What are some leaps of faith you need to take in the near future?

Read and reflect on the following promises made in scripture about God coming through in His time.

24. FOREIGN PRAISE

"When he saw them, he said, 'Go, show yourselves to the priests.' And as they went, they were cleansed. One of them, when he saw he was healed, came back, praising God in a loud voice." (Luke 17:14, 15)

L eave it to the good Dr. Luke to feature a story that no other gospel writer mentions. Parables such as *The Good Samaritan, The Prodigal Son,* and the eyebrow-raising illustration of *The Rich Man* share a common theme (10:29-37; 15; 16:19-31). Almost all of the unique material in Luke have one message the other gospels don't explicitly emphasize: *Jesus is the Christ for the outsider, the forgotten, the overlooked, and the foreigner—for all.*

Most believers would agree that God accepts everyone, however Luke maintains that the outsider is not simply included, but often the shining example. The Centurion's faith is so great Jesus is "amazed" and adds, "I have not found such great faith even in Israel" (Luke 7:1-10). A Syrophoenician woman's persistent devotion demonstrates "great faith" and the parable of *The Good Samaritan* features a Samaritan as the hero.

The message of Luke is not a collection of stories containing subtle hints. There is no innuendo. For example, this week's character of conviction is singled out by two qualities: first his worship, then his nationality. Read the story in Luke 16:11-19 all the way through, then consider a few key insights to reflect on this week.

Insight #1: Leprosy made anyone the ultimate outsider. Anyone with leprosy was literally and socially untouchable. When people were diagnosed with leprosy, the priest declared them "unclean", and their names were taken off of the community record. Lepers were even considered legally dead, which is why they had to see the priest for re-entry into society if they were ever healed. Leprosy provides a perfect analogy to the work of sin.

Insight #2: Jesus knew how to count. If lepers no longer mattered as individuals, Jesus made them significant by noting them, even if it was at a distance. When a band of people hail you from afar, do you count them? Jesus did. Even if leprosy disfigured man's face, the Creator "saw them". In Christ's beautiful mind He saw each individual in turn with singular understanding. When only one returned, Jesus said, "Were not ten healed? Where are the other nine?"

Insight #3: There is a difference between being healed and being made whole. The scripture says that, "as they went, they were cleansed" (Luke 16:14). The word "cleansed" means that the physical problem had been fixed, repaired, and restored. As they made their way, their bodies were made clean from leprosy, but the one who returned received more than physical healing. When the Samaritan leper came back praising God, Jesus told him, "Rise and go; your faith has *made you well*" (Luke 16:19). The word translated as "well" means more than healing, it means being *saved*. His renewal was not simply a physical fix—this *wellness* was eternal.

Insight #4: Restoration is a process. The nine received the gift of more time to live. What they did with their second chance is a mystery, whereas we know from Scripture that the Samaritan leper chose to process his good fortune. First, "he saw that he was healed". All of them noticed their new skin, but only one "saw". The first part of the process is an understanding of the significance of healing. The Samaritan thought about what healing meant. Secondly, the leper returned to the Source instead of racing on to something new. Finally, when the one who returned came "praising God" and "giving thanks", his blessing multiplied.

Insight #5: Don't be surprised to learn the way to life from an outsider. Jesus celebrates the faithfulness of the foreigner who likely never went to Sabbath School and may not have even known the Ten Commandments. Nevertheless, the Samaritan leper becomes the example for all. The bitter hatred between Jews and Samaritans had been fomented for over 500 years. The reason the religious leaders told Jesus in John 8:48, "You are a Samaritan and you have a demon," is they couldn't conceive of a more potent insult. The greatest challenge of the new church in the book of Acts would be to overcome racial hatred in light of the cross.

This week, celebrate the conviction of this unseemly outsider and practice learning from someone you might typically dismiss, or even disdain.

INSIDE OUT

Read the ritual depicted in Leviticus 14 for lepers who were healed. Compare the ceremony to the work of Christ on the cross and look for connections.

Throughout the week choose from one the insights above and apply the message to your life that day.

BEYOND BELIEF

Cool—the word means a temperature not warm or hot, a disposition not friendly, or someone or something that is socially acceptable ("that person is pretty cool!"). Words like "belief", "faith", "opinion", and "idea" all relate to the thoughts a person holds. The difference between a conviction and an opinion has to do with the way a person thinks, commits, and follows through with his or her actions. You will discover a renewed emphasis on the nature and purpose of the Holy Spirit's work in your life, regarding your conscience and the way your life convinces people of God's goodness.

25. CONVERTED AND CONVICTED

"For I am not ashamed of the gospel,
because it is the power of God that brings
salvation to everyone who believes..."
(Romans 1:16)

Examine your life—reflect on the things you think and the things you do that few people really know about. This is not a fishing trip for hidden sins, but a chance to point out aspects of your heart, mind, and life that are not evident to people around you. It is possible to be very familiar with someone and still not really know him or her.

The Bible reveals more about the apostle Paul than any other character, save Jesus. He is described as obligated, eager, and unashamed. Some have Paul pegged as the educated thinker, but if you read what he wrote and what was written about him, clearly there is more to Paul than just a calculating theological mind. Paul describes his previous life in Judaism:

"...how intensely I persecuted the church of God and tried to destroy it. I was advancing in Judaism beyond many of my own age among my people and was extremely zealous for the traditions of my fathers." (Galatians 1:13, 14)

Here again, Paul confesses under oath:

"...in one synagogue after another I used to imprison and beat those who believed in You. And when the blood of Your witness Stephen was being shed, I also was standing by approving, and watching out for the coats of those who were slaying him." (Acts 22:19-20)

Don't let the big theological words fool you; Saul has always been driven by a passion that burns in him like unquenchable flame. Once Saul was converted, the same person that used to be a fanatical legalist became an indomitable champion for the gospel. Paul declares, "For I am *not ashamed* of the gospel, because it is the power of God that brings salvation to everyone who believes" (Romans 1:16; emphasis added). If you had to categorize this brazen apostle's conviction in three statements, perhaps it would be: "I want to *know*, I want to *grow*, and I want to *go*."

Know
Paul explicitly states, "I consider everything a loss because of the surpassing worth of knowing Christ Jesus my Lord," and again adds later in the chapter, "I want to know Christ—yes, to know the power of his resurrection..." (Philippians 3:8, 10). According to Galatians 1:17, Saul hid himself in Arabia for three years after his conversion, likely searching the Scriptures and cultivating this new-found yearning to know the Risen Christ.

Grow
While Paul is a champion of grace, the apostle shows that the mercy of Christ changes, transforms, and grows those who by faith, respond to Christ. Simply listen to his prayer for the church:

"We continually ask God to fill you with the knowledge of his will through all the wisdom and understanding that the Spirit gives, so that you may live a life worthy of the Lord and please him in every way: bearing fruit in every good work, growing in the knowledge of God, being strengthened with all power according to his glorious might so that you may have great endurance and patience..." (Colossians 1:9-11)

Go
Paul was not a calm, quiet Pharisee who sat around thinking and philosophizing. His work possessed him, which is why you see him racing all over the Roman world to preach the gospel. Paul has one speed: Go! "And He said to me, 'Go! For I will send you far away to the Gentiles'" (Acts 22:21).

If your temperament is not like Paul's, know that there are other "heroes of faith" and people of conviction who are equally celebrated and necessary to the family of God. Still, take time this week to imitate the apostle as he invites you to "Follow my example, as I follow the example of Christ" (1 Corinthians 11:1).

INSIDE OUT

Find ways to imitate Paul's passion for the gospel, think about using the three categories of conviction discussed.

26. FAITH YOU CAN'T EXTINGUISH

"A Canaanite woman from that vicinity came to him, crying out, 'Lord, Son of David, have mercy on me! My daughter is demon-possessed and suffering terribly.' Jesus did not answer a word." (Matthew 15:22, 23)

February 22, 1992. The Canadian Province of Alberta, Canada—where the temperature is normally between -20°C to 1°C—saw the temperature skyrocket to a scorching 22.6°C in the dead of winter. On January 19, 1977 it snowed on the town of Homestead, Florida. This city rests on the southern tip of the United States. From July to August in 2010, Russia suffered heat like never before. In some regions the temperature hit the upper 40s (up to 120°F), which claimed the lives of an estimated 15,000 people. And on January 22, in the town of Spearfish, North Dakota, the weather jumped from -20°C to a warm 7°C in the span of two minutes. The anomaly was one of the quickest leaps in temperature recorded.

An anomaly is a rare phenomenon. An inconsistency. A glitch. The encounter between Jesus and the Canaanite woman is an anomaly. Read the whole story in Matthew 15:21-28. *Warning!* If you read the story aloud, you may choke with embarrassment on hearing the way Christ seems to speak to a humble seeker. Even after reading this story dozens of times, you may wish it were written differently, but read on!

When a Canaanite woman cried out for healing for her demon-possessed daughter, Jesus seems to have simply ignored her while the disciples urged Him to get rid of her. When He finally addressed the situation the Lord replied, "I was sent only to the lost sheep of Israel." It's difficult to pass over the way the gospel comes to the world through the people of Israel (Romans 1:16). Consider also that God grants some blessings and good news to the Gentiles, passing over the Jews (Luke 4:25-27). Either way, this story is at offensive at least and at most, cruel. You might be tempted to brush past the harshness of Christ's words and avoid the sick feeling you get in your stomach when you read the exchange. However, to turn away from the story is to ignore the racism—the elitism and the arrogance that stymied the impact of Jews on the surrounding population.

To embrace the truth about the horror of sin is to open a doorway to honor God's solution.

Shift the focus for a moment back to the centerpiece of the story. It's not about the disciples' racism, or the teaching methods of Jesus. The woman is the story. Notice how this snowstorm in summer plays out: "The woman came and knelt before him. 'Lord, help me!' she said. He replied, 'It is not right to take the children's bread and toss it to the dogs.' 'Yes it is, Lord,' she said. 'Even the dogs eat the crumbs that fall from their master's table.' Then Jesus said to her, 'Woman, you have great faith! Your request is granted.' And her daughter was healed at that moment" (Matthew 15:25-28).

She cries out! She comes and kneels. She comes to claim what is rightfully hers. Jesus loved all people with uncharacteristic freedom and never once turned away an honest seeker. This woman sees the game that is played by the world and refuses to play by the same rules. Permit this paraphrase as one explanation of the strange conversation between the mother and Jesus:

"I know your rules, and I know all the prejudices that exist between our nations. I know where many think I stand. According to your people, I am a dog to God. Whether that is true or not, God takes care of dogs, too. More important than an argument on racial divide is my daughter who is possessed by a demon and suffering. I'm willing to be a dog until you, being the Messiah, do what you are supposed to do."

She humbles herself before the full reality of human society and does not allow the petty, sinful state we are in derail her ultimate desire. She claims her spot in the kingdom and, in so doing, claims the King as her own. She does not let prejudice, humiliation, or false assumptions stifle her persevering prayer for her daughter. Finally, the weather returns to normal. As Christ smiles and grants her the gift of healing, the Canaanite mother goes from "dog" at the table to paragon of "great faith". People of conviction have a faith that simply refuses to give up or give in—they persevere.

INSIDE OUT

What is something you believe in that merits unquenchable perseverance?

This week, look for the anomalies in your life. Notice the strange surprises of goodness in people.

27. THE WIDOW'S MIGHT

"As Jesus looked up, he saw the rich putting their gifts into the temple treasury. He also saw a poor widow put in two very small copper coins. 'Truly I tell you,' he said, 'this poor widow has put in more than all the others. '" (Luke 21:1-3)

What do you think is the difference between generosity and charity? How would you differentiate a gift from a donation? In any case, there are a couple of qualities to every act of benevolence: there is the offering and there is the heart of the one who offers it. You can give a large sum of money with a heart of resentment or with joy. A lesser amount may come from a stingy, minimalistic heart or from one open in gratitude. The range of both gift and heart is unlimited, which is why one should be very careful when making observations about either. However, in the story of the widow who gave at the temple, Jesus witnesses a heart so great that the gift is worth celebrating.

The temple courtyard had been set up so different courts divided the areas into which only certain people could go. First, there was the Court of the Gentiles, then there was the Court of Women, and then the Court of Israelites, and finally the Court of the Levites, where the priests would do their work. It was in the Court of Women that 13 offering containers were placed. The offerings were meant to pay for the wood used to burn on the altar, for the incense, for the upkeep of the vessels, and a variety of other temple expenses. The offerings also provided for the basic needs of widows and orphans.

It's true that many of the religious leaders in that day were corrupt. However, the temple service was God's idea, not man's, so withdrawing support was not a meaningful way to protest misuse. The priests being abusive in their leadership didn't undermine the virtue of the entire system. If it is true that money given in offerings rarely made it to orphans and widows, then trust God to know the hearts of people in ways you do not. Jesus accused the religious leadership of His day: "They devour widows' houses and for a show make lengthy prayers. These men will be punished most severely" (Mark 12:40). If the temple was not doing its job taking care of the poor, who would have been more aware of the misuse than this widow? Yet here we have the story recorded in scripture. She was either foolishly unaware or even more impressive than simple words can convey.

Who determines when it's time for God's plans to be complete? Do we decide when the Messiah should come? Do we decide what laws matter and which commands are no longer relevant? Do we decide when a person is truly converted? Do we decide when Jesus will return? Do we decide who is called upon to lead, preach, judge, prophesy, or serve? Don't pity the widow; she gave out of her poverty, and in so doing she demonstrated the true measure of her wealth. She was generous because she was rich—rich in hope. She is like a cool breeze in the stagnant heat of summer or the sight of a flower amid a barren desert. The poor widow is more than refreshing— she is surprising. On paper, her gift is not even a drop in the bucket, but the dent she made in the heart of God moves Jesus to use her generosity as an example to others. Such is the conviction of a generous heart.

The small-hearted big givers gave to be seen. This is the sin of externalism. There are big-hearted givers that give abundantly, generously, and consistently to the work of God and few people are even aware of the details. This is the grace of generosity. Jesus didn't go over and reward her because she had already received her reward. Perhaps the greatest compliment Jesus pays her is to pull His disciples together and use her as an object lesson.

INSIDE OUT

Who in your life does the woman remind you of? If there is any way to communicate a word of appreciation for their big hearts, waste no time in conveying your thoughts to them.

It's not the only time Jesus used a woman's devotion for an object lesson. Read and reflect on another prominent example of great conviction. Luke 10:38-42; Mark 14:1-9

This week, practice giving a gift so valuable that it causes you to live differently.

28. A SENSE OF OUGHT

"As soon as the chief priests and their officials saw him, they shouted, 'Crucify! Crucify!' But Pilate answered, 'You take him and crucify him. As for me, I find no basis for a charge against him'" (John 19:6)

Beyond the sense of sight, smell, touch, taste, hearing, and intuition, now add the *sense of ought*. This sense is different than intuition in that it goes beyond the impulses and impressions that automatically emerge to an embraced ethical framework you believe you should live by. So, are you ready to test your sense of ought?

After serving 5 years of a life sentence, a convicted murderer is freed from prison. After serving 15 years of a life sentence without parole, a man convicted of murdering a family of four is released from incarceration. Also walking the neighborhoods as a free man is one who was convicted of aggravated assault, homicide, and rape. After serving 20 years of a life sentence without parole, he now has a life with new horizons.

When you hear these stories, what is your immediate reaction? Without knowing any more details, there is a *sense of ought* at work in you. A sense of ought is a moral framework that amplifies any ethical discord you see in life. The idea that convicted criminals who were sentenced to life in prison are now living as free men sends a screaming sensation through your mind declaring, "This should not be." What could be worse than someone who is guilty getting set free? Good question. Is there anything worse than the guilty dodging justice? How about being *falsely accused* and sentenced to prison for 5, 15, or 20 years? The detail left out above is that those three examples are men who were falsely convicted based on eyewitness misidentification, false confessions or admissions, inadequate defense, and government misconduct.

The Innocence Project is an organization dedicated to exonerating wrongfully convicted individuals through DNA testing. So far, there have been 336 exonerations from the admission of DNA evidence and the average sentence served for these cases is 14 years. Furthermore, 140 genuine perpetrators have been found as a result of the work of this organization. What causes your sense of ought to enflame more, someone found guilty who is set free on a technicality or an innocent person who is falsely accused and convicted of a crime he or she did not commit?

If you are guilty and you get away with a crime, there is at least an expectation that "you reap what you sow" and somehow justice will make its way around to meet you, even if it comes at the end. If you are accused of doing something you never did, something about that level of injustice makes it so much more wrong.

When you look at the Jewish legal process, you can see it was designed to protect the innocent from being wrongly accused, even if it meant setting the guilty free. The Sanhedrin consisted of 70 elders with the high priest presiding. Any capital case required two to three witnesses for condemnation (Deuteronomy 17:6). The witnesses were examined separately while the accused held to be absolutely innocent until witnesses were confirmed and stated. Any witness had to be present from the beginning to the end. Finally, if there was a conviction for which you were a witness, you had to throw the first stone. It was illegal to try any person at night, on the day before the Sabbath, or the day before a religious festival. Why? With capital cases they always wanted an extra day for reflection if the verdict was guilty and they did not want to be putting people to death on the Sabbath. Now, consider the trials of Jesus against the backdrop of what *ought to* have happened. Trials typically have at least two purposes: to discover the truth and to establish justice.

Conviction and the sense of ought are not developed in trials, but rather revealed by it. During the arrest and trial, the disciples flee, the crowds riot, and the religious leaders compromise the law to condemn Jesus to death. In all of this, Jesus remains the same. As you open your eyes to justice and cultivate your sense of ought, may the Spirit of truth strengthen your heart this week.

INSIDE OUT

In what areas of your life do you want a more sensitive conscience?

Read and reflect on Isaiah 53 and consider the cost of justice and the gift of grace.

Read the various trials of Christ and examine the way the conscience of different characters are either seared or awakened.
- Matthew 26:57-27:26
- Mark 14:53-15:15
- Luke 22:66-23:25
- John 18:19-19:16

29. PARENTHETICALLY SPEAKING

"Indeed, when Gentiles, who do not have the law, do by nature things required by the law, they are a law for themselves, even though they do not have the law. They show that the requirements of the law are written on their hearts, their consciences also bearing witness, and their thoughts sometimes accusing them and at other times even defending them."
(Romans 2:14, 15)

A re you a glass half-empty or a glass half-full kind of person? The assumption is that every person is either one or the other, but most people would agree that the distinction is not always clear. Nevertheless, there is a tendency to place people in basic categories. If you had to divide the world into two groups, how would you separate them? Paul, for practical purposes, divided people into two groups: Jews and Gentiles. Even though Jews received the Law of God and Gentiles did not, both groups are going to be judged fairly in the end. How is this possible? Did the Jews have an advantage? Yes. God chose them and revealed to them His plan for salvation. *The Plan* even included the Son of God becoming a human, as a Jewish-born man! How is that fair? *Fair is not always equal treatment,* so God will hold those who had The Law to one standard, and those who did not have access to another. What other standard is there?

It is important to remember that before God issued the Ten Commandments from Sinai there was already a "sense" or a natural agreement that killing runs counter to the will of God. For instance, when Cain killed his brother Abel, God did not point to commandment number six and refer Cain to "the law". Instead, God said, "Why are you *angry?* Why is your face downcast? If you do what is *right,* will you not be accepted? But if you do not do what is right, sin is crouching at your door; it desires to have you, but you must rule over it" (Genesis 4:6, 7; emphasis added).

God addresses the anger and the immorality of Cain's mind-set, which is what Jesus ultimately did in the Sermon on the Mount (Matthew 5:21, 22). The laws given to the Jews were to be shared with the world through their own practice. In essence, they were to witness to the world God's character and plan for all people. You don't need the laws in written format to know whether something is right or wrong.

Think about this! How many people have lived on this planet who had no access to the Law of God or the Bible? How will they who have gone to sleep be judged? You are responsible for what you were *able to know.* To stubbornly resist or apathetically ignore what God has revealed to you does not provide you with a valid excuse for the way you choose to live. The big question for all people is, "Did your heart and life correspond to what you were able to know?" Paul is saying that there is an unwritten law within the human heart. Can that heart get bruised, damaged, and scarred so much that one may no longer sense the truth written into the "image of God" as revealed through the creation of humanity? Yes. The un-written law is more than common sense or human instinct. It has to do with the conscience. The law works in us all as a principle that postures people to choose to obey it or discard it for another law.

Some describe this law as a voice that speaks to you about right and wrong. For all that we still don't know about the conscience, you can rest confidently that God's ultimate will is for you to respond to Him as Creator, Father, Savior, Teacher, and Friend. May God's presence and truth be revealed to you this week.

INSIDE OUT

Below are several ways to respond to God this week and passages from Scripture to guide you. Think, pray, and talk about God with your friends and co-workers.

30. A CONSCIENCE EYE

*"For since the creation of the world God's
invisible qualities—his eternal power and
divine nature—have been clearly seen, being
understood from what has been made,
so that people are without excuse."
(Romans 1:20)*

How do you clearly see something invisible? In this conversation with
Paul about conviction and the human conscience, it's easy to get a
headache. First of all, what is the wrath of God and how does it relate
to the love of God? Secondly, how is God's power and nature revealed by
looking at the created world?

Wrath of God
The apostle Paul uses the word "wrath" nine times in the book of Romans.
Strangely, some are tempted to interpret "God's wrath" as His angry
hand seeking vengeance—or at least justice. If you read all the passages
containing the word "wrath" in Romans, you get the sense that the wrath
of God is a process and a result. In 1 John 5:11, John echoes this principle,
saying, "Whoever has the Son has life; whoever does not have the Son of
God does not have life." There is no meanness, only the reality of life with
God or life without God. Life without God leads to life *as if I am God,* which
does not end well. Wrath can be described as God *letting us go off to do what
we want more than anything else.*

In this world there are rules, principles, and examples of cause and effect.
Sin breaks down to death. Plant your seed in the field too late and your
crop fails. Ignore the laws of physics when you build a house and your
building will fall to pieces. Neglect the rules of health and you will suffer
disease. If you decide to align with God in a grace-filled relationship, your
life will follow into eternity. If you should choose to defy the laws of life
and go your own way, the wrath of God (God letting you go) will come to its
rightful end.

Seeing God's Hand and Face
Even if you have never heard of Moses, Jesus, or Esther, Paul would say, "No

one can say, 'I didn't know.'" Look at the world! See how it is constructed! The earth is the exact size, located in the right place, and turning at a perfect rate for life to exist. Examine a bird's feather, the behavior of animals, or the complexity of a cell and there is evidence for wonder. Consider what others said about creation:

David: "When I consider your heavens, the work of your fingers, the moon and the stars, which you have set in place, what is mankind that you are mindful of them, human beings that you care for them?" (Psalm 8:3, 4)

John: "Worthy are you, our Lord and God, to receive glory and honor and power, for you created all things, and by your will they existed and were created." (Revelation 4:11)

Job: "But ask the animals, and they will teach you, or the birds in the sky, and they will tell you; or speak to the earth, and it will teach you, or let the fish in the sea inform you. Which of all these does not know that the hand of the LORD has done this?" (Job 12:7-9)

Observing the created world does not "explain" the nature of God, but compels you to seek Him. Do you wonder what kind of God could make this world? Know that God's love leaves no stone unturned when it comes to saving people. There will be countless numbers of people who did not know John 3:16, but saw the sun dawn in the morning and sensed the hand of God at work. There are many who have never heard the story of Jesus, but their eyes witness the wonder of birth and their hearts lift up to the Creator in gratitude. Only God knows.

As you live a life of worship this week, watch carefully, in awe of the Creator's hand at work and His wonderful face smiling on His children.

INSIDE OUT

There are many passages that describe the glory of God in creation. Some are listed below for further reading. These are just a few, so intentionally seek out and watch for God's "invisible qualities" and "divine nature" in the world around you this week.
- Psalm 19:1
- Hebrews 11:1, 2
- Isaiah 37:16
- Jeremiah 32:17

This week, pray for those you know or come in contact with who are looking for something else in the world other than their Creator.

31. THE SPIRIT OF CONVICTION (PART 1)

"But very truly I tell you, it is for your good that I am going away. Unless I go away, the Advocate will not come to you; but if I go, I will send him to you. When he comes, he will prove the world to be in the wrong about sin and righteousness and judgment..."
(John 16:7, 8)

Do you ever hide from conversations that you know you don't have the energy for? This book is on Christian conviction and while this subject matter could never be exhausted in one book, it is not right to meander through the scriptures without mentioning the Holy Spirit. It's even more difficult to discuss the Holy Spirit and not consider the Trinity. It is nearly impossible to start a conversation about the Holy Spirit knowing that whatever you think and say will fall short. In a way it feels a little like quicksand: the more you agitate and move, the faster and deeper you sink.

Still, the words Jesus spoke about the Holy Spirit are too important to omit, so it is safer to just dive in. This week the focus is on the nature of the Holy Spirit and part two is on the specific work of the Spirit according to Jesus. In the following verses Jesus is preparing His disciples for some pivotal moments ahead. Imagine having the following statements dropped on you in one conversation:

"I am going there to prepare a place for you. And if I go and prepare a place for you, I will come back and take you to be with me that you also may be where I am." (John 14:1-3)

"Very truly I tell you, whoever believes in me will do the works I have been doing, and they will do even greater things than these, because I am going to the Father." (John 14:12)

"You heard me say, 'I am going away and I am coming back to you.' If you loved me, you would be glad that I am going to the Father, for the Father is greater than I." (John 14:28)

"All this I have told you so that you will not fall away. They will put you out of the synagogue; in fact, the time is coming when anyone who kills you will think they are offering a service to God." (John 16:2)

That is a lot to process. "I'm leaving. I'll come back to get you later. Do what I was doing. Actually, now that I'm gonna be gone, do greater things than even I did. I'm sending you a 'Helper'. Love each other—even if it means dying. The world may hate you—I know how you feel. You will be persecuted by people who think killing you is doing God a favor. You may be tempted to quit, but don't." The Holy Spirit is everywhere, in everyone, all at the same time. Though God the Son came to earth in human form, the Trinity are spiritual beings. In the same way that God the Son had a mission on earth, coming to humanity as Jesus the Messiah, the Holy Spirit has a specific job to do as well.

While it's a theological truth that we were made in the image of God, it is also healthy to maintain an awareness of how God is unlike everything else we think we know. You may know how to drive a car and you have a sense that your knowledge is exhaustive, or close to it. You know that 2 + 2 = 4 and your interpretation of that equation is complete. By now, you should know that men are different from women and an ear is not a toe. You can confidently say you know these things, but not so with God.

Many find it difficult to claim they know God because there is far more they don't know about God than what they do know. Still, Jesus simply stated, "to know God is eternal life" (John 17:3). Certainly God doesn't try to make knowing Him impossible, or even difficult; it's simply hard to know the Divine the same way we know everything else. Herein lies the tension between explaining something and experiencing it. You can know God personally, but not entirely, and while you cannot fully explain the Trinity, you are able to experience a relationship with God that is meaningful.

INSIDE OUT

Refresh your mind with passages that give insight into the nature and purpose of the Trinity.
- Matthew 28:19
- 1 Corinthians 12:4-6
- 2 Corinthians 13:14
- Ephesians 4:4-7
- 1 Peter 1:2
- Jude 20-21

32. THE SPIRIT OF CONVICTION (PART 2)

"He will prove the world to be in the wrong about sin and righteousness and judgment." (John 16:8)

Whenever you hear the Trinity listed, there is an order. You would never hear of someone baptized "in the name of the Jesus, the Holy Spirit, and the Father". Why? While there are three distinct persons collectively referred to as "God", there does seem to be an order. The Father is first, because the Son is "begotten" from the Father (John 3:16). The Son is second in the order because the Son describes the arrival of the Holy Spirit as the result of His own ascension (John 14:12). The Holy Spirit comes from the Father (John 15:26). According to 1 John 4:10, it was the Father who sent the Son and they both sent the Holy Spirit (John 14:26). Clearly God the Father is the Creator, The Son is the Redeemer, and the Holy Spirit is the one who empowers and sanctifies people (Isaiah 44:24; Galatians 3:13; Romans 15:16).

Now, just when you think you have God's nature cleanly delineated, you read that Jesus is also the Creator (John 1:1-3; Colossians 1:16; 1 Corinthians 8:6). The Spirit was also active at the creation (Genesis 1:2) and at work in the children of Israel (Exodus 35:30-35). King David pleaded with God: "take not your Holy Spirit from me" (Psalms 51:11). If the above doesn't start feeling like quicksand, add to the equation that "Christ was that rock" for the Israelites in the desert (1 Corinthians 10:4). Again, God and His infinite nature will not fit in your head, but He does promise to take up residence in your heart. However, first you must be convinced that you need God.

The word John used to convey the work of the Holy Spirit is translated "convict" or "convince". It was mainly used to describe the legal exercise of cross-examining someone. The word also carries the idea of stirring people's consciences until they come to see clearly their own error in a way they have not perceived before. Combine the words "convict" and "convince" and you capture one of the primary works of the Holy Spirit.

When in your life have you experienced conviction? It may have been a sin you cherished or a deed you didn't really regard as "wrong". Conviction can come gradually like the dawn, where the sin becomes more and more apparent or it can pour down suddenly and all at once, like a tropical rainstorm. Either way, conviction is how you become convinced of your wrongness and unmistakable need.

Jesus informed the disciples that the Holy Spirit would convict the world about sin, righteousness, and judgment. When used today, those three words often cause people to cringe. It's very unpopular to talk about sin because to identify something as such is seen as being "judgmental". And when someone or something is "righteous", it comes across as aloof at best, or holier-than-thou at worst. Don't get the conversation started about "judgment" or "judging others" because, in the eyes of secular culture today, being "non-judgmental" is more highly valued than being honest, kind or faithful. Isn't it interesting to realize the work of the Holy Spirit is what current secular culture demonizes?

The first area the Holy Spirit spends effort is convicting you of sin. There are sins and there is Sin. When we mention the plural sins, we're referring to decisions made and actions taken that "miss the mark"; it is a phrase for the times we achieve what is not in harmony with God's will or God's way. Sin with a capital S is the universal spiritual condition that causes a broken relationship with God. The second area of the heart that the Holy Spirit targets is righteousness—the state of right-being and right-doing. It is not simply someone who does good works, but someone who does good because they are good. The Spirit of Christ awakens in people a consciousness of their sin by contrast with the righteousness of Christ. According to Matthew, the centurion at the cross declared, "Surely this was man was righteous" (Matthew 27:54).

The third area the Holy Spirit focuses on is the reality of judgment. When you know that there will be a moment in which you will have to account for your choices, the power of that awareness can move you to make important ones. Judgment is coming to everyone and you will either be graded on your own deeds or you will trust that Christ's righteousness covers you. This week, welcome the work of the Holy Spirit in you.

INSIDE OUT

As you pray this week, consider the promised work of the Holy Spirit and ask specifically for what the Spirit intends to give.

33. POSTURING CONVICTION

"At dawn he appeared again in the temple courts, where all the people gathered around him, and he sat down to teach them." (John 8:2)

In this story, we read of the posture Jesus assumed when He responded to the accusers and the adulterous woman. This encounter occurs at dawn when people would gather for the Morning Prayer and teaching. In Jesus's day it was customary to stand up to read scripture and sit down to offer commentary on the words that were spoken. They stood while the Word of God was being read and sat while people talked about it in order to make a deliberate statement that scripture was more authoritative than anything people might say. Jesus sat. As Jesus sat, the frenzied mob of accusers interrupted His teaching.

"The teachers of the law and the Pharisees brought in a woman caught in adultery. They made her stand before the group and said to Jesus, 'Teacher, this woman was caught in the act of adultery. In the Law Moses commanded us to stone such women. Now what do you say?' They were using this question as a trap, in order to have a basis for accusing him" (John 8:3-6).

This story has so many unanswered questions; for example, where were the required witnesses (Deuteronomy 17:6; 19:15)? Furthermore, where was the other guilty party? According to the law of God "both the adulterer and the adulteress shall be put to death" (Leviticus 20:10). And, how was it that religious leaders could be privy to the secret sins of others at sunrise? This whole story screams out that the scene was a set up, but nonetheless, she was guilty. She stood before the crowd. Jesus sat.

Know that this trial was not about the woman, but was instead a trial of Jesus. She was only collateral damage. This was not the Sanhedrin. Her case would never make it to trial for the death penalty because Pilate did not care whether she or any other woman was an adulteress. She had only broken a Jewish law and due to their subjugation to Roman power, the Jews had no authority to do what they are doing—it was a total sham! If He upheld the Law of Moses, His reputation as a friend of sinners would be finished. If He dismissed the Law of Moses, Jesus would easily be dismissed as the Messiah. Jesus changed His posture. The Messiah no longer sat—now He stooped.

"But Jesus bent down and started to write on the ground with his finger. When they kept on questioning him, he straightened up and said to them, 'Let any one of you who is without sin be the first to throw a stone at her.' Again he stooped down and wrote on the ground" (John 8:6-8).

Jesus gets low in the dirt. He stoops to wash feet. You can't pick up a child while standing straight—you have to stoop low to catch kids in your arms. The Savior stoops down to scoop some mud for the eyes of a boy blind from birth. He stoops to write in the dirt. No one knows what Jesus wrote, but the impact of it speaks volumes. Common knowledge tells us that people sharply accuse others of the very things they do in secret. If this is any indication of human behavior, we can imagine that while Jesus writes, the rocks drop, and the saints leave the courtyard like a bunch of sinners who have some thinking to do. Jesus stoops to write in the dirt until everyone is gone—then He straightens up.

"At this, those who heard began to go away one at a time, the older ones first, until only Jesus was left, with the woman still standing there. Jesus straightened up and asked her, 'Woman, where are they? Has no one condemned you?' 'No one, sir,' she said. 'Then neither do I condemn you,' Jesus declared. 'Go now and leave your life of sin'" (John 8:9-11).

Judgment is between you and God. No crowds. No outside opinions. No committees. Jesus clears this court to give the woman the good news by asking her an easy question: "Where are your accusers?" The answer is so obvious, but the meaning is monumental! "Has no one condemned you?" She was guilty. She was an adulteress. The only way Jesus could let her go is if someone else paid and someone else behaved righteously for her. The only one who had the right to condemn her straightens up and sets her free.

INSIDE OUT

Mirror the different postures Jesus practiced. Sit and submit to God's word. Think and listen for ways to apply what God is trying to say to you today. Stoop low this week and get your hands dirty on behalf of someone else—someone who has no one defending them. And stand up for someone. Stand up, not based on their wrong-doing, but on God's grace—God's right doing on their behalf.

34. CEASE AND RESPOND

"'Brothers, what shall we do?' Peter replied, 'Repent and be baptized, every one of you, in the name of Jesus Christ for the forgiveness of your sins. And you will receive the gift of the Holy Spirit.'" (Acts 2:37, 38)

When doctors want to see inside your body, they take an X-ray, an MRI or a CT scan to detect if something is amiss or intact. Can you imagine if there were a way to examine the course of your life in a similar manner? What would be revealed? Some of the wisest people on the planet take time to reflect and think about the past, present, and future. Even more, such people will often press themselves to consider what is meaningful about the events they experience. If you were to X-ray the hearts of people who negotiate life well, you would see the marks of pinpricks—evidence of the various moments when their hearts suffered a substantial poke from the Spirit of God.

If you are too busy to stop and think about what matters most and what should be first in your life, you might miss much needed "pinpricks" to your heart and your conscience. However, when you make a point of slowing down to dwell on the importance of eternal things versus temporary things, *you give God access to do what is needed*. Think about your own story and take a mental X-ray of the moments when spiritual awakening occurred. Did revival come to you in the flurry of being busy or did you have to set everything else aside for a moment to "see the light"?

When God set His people on the road to the Promised Land, He gave them a calendar of appointments to stop and remember pivotal truths. These events were called "Sabbaths"; the word "Sabbath" means to stop or cease. In addition to the seventh-day Sabbath set aside at creation, God added several festivals that would tell the story of salvation—if the people would stop and pay attention to it. The monumental event was Passover, where grace was granted to the people of God in the story of judgment. When people hear of "judgment" they usually become anxious, but the point of Passover was to experience being judged "not guilty" and "righteous" because of the Lamb. You can read the details about these "sabbaths" in Leviticus 23, but the big picture is that God's intention for the calendar was to posture His people in such a way as to have their hearts and minds arrested.

God placed on the Pentecost, or the Feast of Weeks, fifty days after Passover. This was a time to reflect on God's Law revealed on Mt. Sinai and what it meant in their relationships with others. If you think about the Law of God, you know that the first four laws address the relationship between you and God, and the last six focus on your relationship with others: revelation and community.

Fifty days after the cross the believers stopped their work, gathered together to make themselves available to God. If any disciple knows what it's like to have the heart pricked, it would be Peter. Fifty days after the fog lifted and the dust settled, Peter sees the past, present, and future with greater clarity. His sermon "pricked the hearts" of the people who gathered and they asked, "What shall we do?" You may recall that the word "repent" simply means "to change your mind". So much of what God seeks to do in people begins with an internal transformation that becomes evident on the outside.

"Therefore, I urge you, brothers and sisters, in view of God's mercy, to offer your bodies as a living sacrifice, holy and pleasing to God—this is your true and proper worship. Do not conform to the pattern of this world, but be transformed by the renewing of your mind. Then you will be able to test and approve what God's will is—his good, pleasing and perfect will" (Romans 12:1, 2).

When the people heard the story of Jesus in light of the plan of salvation, their hearts were "pricked" in an unforgettable way. Today, the same Holy Spirit seeks to have access to your heart. Your task is to be still and respond.

INSIDE OUT

This week read and reflect on the cross. Each day make a note of what pricks your heart. Reflect over the last three years and retrace some of the moments your heart was "pricked". This week, talk to others about some of the pivotal moments you recall and stir past convictions in your heart today.

OF CONSCIENCE AND CONFIDENCE

Throughout the Bible you will see and hear people confidently speak their minds, and in some cases, their lives. It is sobering to see how the conscience can be a conduit for God's grace, but is vulnerable enough to become seared. The practice and process of drawing close to God over time develops an attitude of confidence that is unmistakable. In this section you will learn how to deepen your relationship with God in a way that establishes your place in God's presence. Walking with God is matter of living by certain convictions and considering how to experience that walk is one of the deepest joys of life.

35. A GOOD CONSCIENCE

"Such teachings come through hypocritical liars, whose consciences have been seared as with a hot iron." (1 Timothy 4:2)

How do you relate to the people who share the "honest truth" with you? If you are struggling with the phrase "honest truth" because you think the truth should always be honest and never need qualification, then you are not alone. However, you also know that it is common for people to modulate how they express their thoughts so as not to be offensive or alarming. As people err on the side of being "politically correct", they often fail to be clear and end up speaking a lot of words, but saying nothing. The reasons why this impulse has become so prevalent in our society are a separate topic, but right now we're going to focus on the fact that despite the trend, there are still those who will risk offending people they care about in order to tell them the truth.

Paul's final words to Timothy are about guarding his conscience. Have you ever wondered what it means to have a "seared conscience"? From a technical standpoint, something that is seared signifies it is so badly damaged by fire that the nerve endings are dead and the tissue scars over. As a result, you can't feel pain or anything else in that part of the body. The faithful mentor urges Timothy to care for his conscience—it can be seared. The message is basically: "Even you can lose your faith and fall away." Clearly, Paul is not seeking to motivate the young pastor by fear, but because "shipwrecking your faith" is a subtle work that sneaks up on you, the counsel given is not so subtle.

In fact, there is a difference in being moved by fear and being motivated by it. Like being splashed with cold water while you are sleeping or surprised by a horn as you drive, the shock moves you from passive complacency to an acute awareness. The immediate fear causes you to adjust, assess, and make changes. Being moved by fear can be helpful, but being motivated by fear is destructive. When fear freezes you in a perpetual state of shock, you don't see well enough to make good decisions. Fear can nudge you to a better way or it can paralyze your mind. It is never God's plan that anyone should live in a consistent state of fear. In fact, the scripture is clear about this:

- "Even though I walk through the darkest valley, I will fear no evil, for you are with me; your rod and your staff, they comfort me." (Psalm 23:4)

- "There is no fear in love. But perfect love drives out fear, because fear has to do with punishment. The one who fears is not made perfect in love." (1 John 4:18)
- "For the Spirit God gave us does not make us timid (fear), but gives us power, love and self-discipline." (2 Timothy 1:7)

God's Spirit longs to walk with you and within you, but will never oppress you into obedience. In the same way that physical pain warns the body of danger, the conscience is the function of your mind that moves you to pay attention to the truths you know. What is more dangerous than pain? To be unable to feel pain when something is harming you. This is what Paul means by warning Timothy about people who have a seared conscience. How does this "searing" happen?
- Stubbornly refuse to listen and learn
- Substitute contempt and criticism for patient concern
- Minimize attitudes and behaviors you know are wrong
- Delay the choices and changes you know are necessary in your life
- Postpone the need to act with integrity and courage today
- Demean those who are trying to do what you
  know deep down you should be doing, too

This week, take care of your conscience; examine your heart and mind in a way that falls fully on the grace of God, striving for the promise of renewal.

INSIDE OUT

Reflect on recent moments when your conscience spoke to you. What was the message and how did you respond?

What biblical characters can you recall who seemed to have their conscience seared (or close to it)? What did they do and fail to do along the way?

Read about the people just prior to the flood in Genesis 6:5. In what way is your culture like this and in what way is it different?

36. FULLY PERSUADED

"Yet he did not waver through unbelief regarding the promise of God, but was strengthened in his faith and gave glory to God, being fully persuaded that God had power to do what he had promised."
(Romans 4:20, 21)

If you're reading this book, it's likely you have lived long enough to know that some people keep their promises and some don't. Also, there are many levels of to the idea of keeping a promise. For example, to say, "I'll meet you in the library" or "I will come and help you this afternoon" is a very low level promise. If for some reason the person doesn't show up, you may not initially question his or her word, especially if an emergency derailed the plans or something beyond control delayed the person. However, if missing appointments becomes a pattern, then over time you will inevitably question whether that person's word is dependable.

To say, "I promise to love, honor and cherish you, in sickness and in health... for as long as I live..." is another kind of promise. A vow is obviously more sacred and more significant than a spoken agreement to meet someone at the library, but even still, the pattern of keeping your word is key to being known as a reliable person. The Bible says that Noah walked with God, David was a man after God's own heart, and the Messiah would be a prophet like Moses. Even though you can cite glaring moments of weakness in the lives of Noah, David, and Moses, the overall pattern of their lives still stands.

If people are considered reliable because they keep their word more often than not, how much more dependable is God's unfailing word? How has God kept His promises to you over the course of your life? What promises remain that God has yet to fulfill? Consider a few of the most famous biblical promises and ask, "Which has God answered and which are yet to be realized?"

- "But my God shall supply all your need according to his riches in glory by Christ Jesus." (Philippians 4:19)

- "My grace is sufficient for you." (2 Corinthians 12:9)
- "If we confess our sins, he is faithful and just and will forgive us our sins and purify us from all unrighteousness." (1 John 1:9)
- "But seek first his kingdom and his righteousness, and all these things will be given to you as well." (Matthew 6:33)

Abraham could say confidently that God is a promise keeper. Abraham was called to "go to a land he did not know" and started walking. Abraham believed the promise that he would become the father of a great nation. Abraham trusted that God would provide a Savior. Abraham, although not flawless in his choices, chose to bank everything on a promise that would not be realized in his lifetime. Still, Paul describes Abraham as being "fully persuaded that God had power to do what He promised".

The bedrock of your relationship to God is grounded on whether you, like Abraham, are convinced God will do what He promises. Do you trust God? If any of your Christian convictions endure, it is likely because you simply believe God will not let you down. Even though there are moments in your life when your certainty wanes or your doubts tend to ebb and flow, if you can say that more often than not "God's promises are sure," then you are in good company.

As you venture out into a week that may appear normal, may God's extraordinary grace enable you to see that His word is true and His promises are reliable.

INSIDE OUT

Think of the surfaces you walk on every day. The floor in your house, the sidewalk or path you walk on every day, the steps you walk up and down. How reliable are the places where you put your feet? Are you absolutely certain they will hold? How much more reliable is God's character—His promise-keeping ways? Are there areas of your life you trust God with explicitly and some you struggle to turn over to Him?

This week, pay attention to what you stand on and compare the structures under your feet to the truth that God will always keep His promises.

37. APPROACH WITH CONFIDENCE

*"Therefore, since we have a great
high priest who has ascended into heaven,
Jesus the Son of God, let us hold firmly to the
faith we profess.... Let us then approach God's
throne of grace with confidence, so that we
may receive mercy and find grace to
help us in our time of need."*
(Hebrews 4:14-16)

When in your life have you ever received a "pep-talk"? If you have ever witnessed an athletic coach attempt to move a team to peak-performance before a game, then you will recognize one of the Bible's best pep-talks. "You have a sympathetic high priest!" This statement invites you to relate to God with freedom, confidence, and peace. A pep-talk launches the team toward the intended goal. Why come boldly to your sympathetic high priest? The goal is to "receive mercy and find grace to help when you need it"!

How can this be true? How can Jesus intimately know you and your sinful state, and still be the Holy Son of God? Consider how Jesus was "tempted in every way, as we are…" by reading Luke 4:1-13; also note how His temptations differ from ours. What is the nature of Christ? In a world where people hunger for a God who identifies with them, the nature of Jesus is relevant on at least two levels: 1) emotionally—that Jesus feels what you feel enables Him to be a sympathetic friend, and 2) redemptively—that Jesus experienced the battle you face and won is what enables His righteousness to be given to you. Surely no one short of Jesus could sacrifice for humanity and satisfy justice. Only the Creator could make Himself the Incarnate One—a creature.

Jesus was fully human and fully divine. If you can't understand this, you are not alone. You can walk away because you aren't able to fully comprehend it, or you can let the implications of this fundamental truth compel you to Him. Jesus experienced temptation as we do, in that He was tempted by what is in Him. When you walk along the trail, you are likely not tempted to look at a rock and think, "I'm so hungry! That rock would make an amazing cookie!" Why? It's not in you to speak to a rock and change it. Jesus was hungry—in that way He is like you. Since He could use His divinity to meet physical needs it was tempting, but here is where your temptations and His are different. Your temptations come from a nature that is broken by sin and bent toward selfishness; the temptations of Christ target the impulse of God's Son to save humanity.

Likely, you are not tempted to leap down from a tall building as marketing ploy to make yourself credible to the masses. Clearly, since you are not able to possess the entire world by surrendering to Satan, it's not a choice you are tempted to make. And again, you don't feel the internal pull to turn rocks into curry and rice. You and Jesus know the temptation—the pull. In fact, it can be said that Jesus is more keenly aware of temptation and more fully tempted than you are. You give in to temptation before you are even aware you are being tempted. Not so with Jesus. In this way, He is different. He is "The Only Begotten, The Word that became Flesh, The Firstborn of Creation, The Son of Man and The Son of God". His knowledge of humanity is sharper and more intimate than anyone else born of a woman.

If you find that trying to explain the nature of Jesus only gets more difficult the more you try, examine that conundrum. Either this Jesus is a contradictory equation with no true answer, or He is God in the flesh. You will not contain God in your brain. You will not reach far enough to grab the edges of His existence. You cannot comprehend His Majesty, but you can come to Him today and Jesus will know and understand you.

INSIDE OUT

Are there moments when you feel more or less comfortable with approaching God in prayer? What causes you to approach God hesitantly? What circumstances or attitudes in your life make drawing near to God problematic? Is it fear? Apathy? Shame? If you were to take this "pep-talk" to heart, what would you expect to change in your walk with God?

Read the following stories where Jesus was severely tempted and reflect on how His struggle is similar to yours as well as how it is different.
- Luke 4:1-13
- Matthew 4:1-11
- Matthew 26:36-46
- Matthew 27:39, 40

38. DRAW NEAR

"...let us draw near to God with a sincere heart and with the full assurance that faith brings, having our hearts sprinkled to cleanse us from a guilty conscience and having our bodies washed with pure water."
(Hebrews 10:22)

Some children take their time warming up to new people when they first meet them. While there are kids who are exceptions to this tendency, the little ones usually keep their distance until they are comfortable enough to approach. The same dynamic occurs with animals that have been mistreated or even adults who have experienced disappointment— until you feel safe, you approach with caution. Have you ever wondered why so many people tend to keep God at a distance? In the same way you may possess a conviction to pray, serve, or be kind, some are convicted to approach God with caution. Do you remember the first impulse Adam and Eve experienced after sinning in the garden?

"Then the man and his wife heard the sound of the Lord God as he was walking in the garden in the cool of the day, and they hid from the Lord God among the trees of the garden. But the Lord God called to the man, 'Where are you?' He answered, 'I heard you in the garden, and I was afraid because I was naked; so I hid'" (Genesis 3:8-10).

Where are you? Drawing close or keeping your distance? According to Hebrews, two truths make the invitation possible: "Since we have confidence to enter the Most Holy Place by the blood of Jesus, by a new and living way opened for us through the curtain, that is, his body, and since we have a great priest over the house of God..." (Hebrews 10:19-21). By the blood of Jesus and the ministry of the High Priest anyone can make their way to God with confidence. The dividing veil is gone. Your sin once separated you from God and sentenced you to death, but the blood of Christ changes everything. Your debt is paid. Because of Christ, you are clean. In Christ, you are righteous. With Christ, you may come boldly to God as child. And yet, it seems so natural to resist—to hesitate.

If you are not "assured in your heart" that this message is true, but you suspect it might be— you hesitate. If you are sure about God, but not sure about your own sincerity—you hesitate. Like Adam and Eve hiding in the bushes: they don't run away, but they can't draw near either, until God invites them. In the conversation, painful as it may be, the distance closes and the children of Eden draw near. Many "believers" pause and linger at a distance because faith is not something you gain in an instant. Add to the problem how easy it is doubt God's mercy when you doubt your own sincerity, as though God's grace mirrors your devotion. No way!

God's grace opens the way for you to freely learn how to love Him. Your unfaithfulness does not cancel out God's grace. Embracing the mercy of God is something those who would draw near to God learn to do. If this message is difficult for you to accept, know that you are not alone. If you read the book of Hebrews, you will find a letter written to a bunch of fellow believers who feel anxious, fearful, and unconfident. Still, all are called to "come close to God".

- "Let us draw near with confidence to the throne of grace, that we may receive mercy and may find grace to help in time of need." (Hebrews 4:16)
- "He is able to save forever those who draw near to God through Him, since He always lives to make intercession for them." (Hebrews 7:25)

The beauty displayed in the heavenly sanctuary is that Jesus has opened the way of full access to God by His blood. Do you sense God inviting you to draw near today? Don't worry if you don't do it well at first; you will learn.

INSIDE OUT

As you pray, meditate on the assurance in James 4:8 that "as you draw near to God, He will draw near to you." How would you practice this as you pray?

Throughout the day, pause to think about the work Christ did for you at Calvary and what He is doing for you now in heaven.

Are there parts of your life you keep at a distance from God? What are some things you never talk about in prayer that you should? Practice drawing close and trusting the intimacy of His nearness.

39. SOMEONE

*"And of this gospel I was appointed
a herald and an apostle and a teacher. That
is why I am suffering as I am. Yet this is no
cause for shame, because I know whom I have
believed, and am convinced that he is able to
guard what I have entrusted to him until
that day." (2 Timothy 1:11, 12)*

One of the most significant shifts you will ever make regarding your convictions is the move from believing something to believing Someone. *It is entirely possible for you to get the point of the Bible and still miss the Person.* It is possible to embrace Christianity and avoid the Christ. As Paul senses that his life on earth is heading toward an inevitable conclusion, his words are not focused on theological truths such as grace, sin, justification, the law, hope, or atonement. Paul declares the only truth that matters in the final moments of life—Jesus. To say, "I know in whom I have believed" conveys a noble thought to all: it's Someone, not something. The Subject of Scripture is more than a history, more tangible than a lesson or a moral belief. You can make a list of all the notions you believe to be true, but there's really only *one who is The Truth.*

Jesus told the Pharisees, "You study the Scriptures diligently because you think that in them you have eternal life. These are the very Scriptures that testify about me, yet you refuse to come to me to have life." (John 5:39-40) If you were facing your final moments of your life, what would be your statement?

Imagine having a birthday party where friends and family gathered from all over the country to celebrate. What if they enjoyed food, played games, ate cake and ice cream, and then packed up and left without ever acknowledging the reason for the occasion? Depending on whether they left gifts and some cake, you would be disappointed because a birthday should be about making "someone" feel special. While suffering in prison is not the party Paul would choose, his mind is stayed on the one he suffered for—knowing Christ was enough for him.

Perhaps one of the most disturbing things Jesus ever said had to do with who you know. "Not everyone who says to Me, 'Lord, Lord,' will enter the kingdom of heaven, but he who does the will of My Father who is in heaven will enter. Many will say to Me on that day, 'Lord, Lord, did we not prophesy in Your name, and in Your name cast out demons, and in Your name perform many miracles?' And then I will declare to them, 'I never knew you'" (Matthew 7:21-23). Not only will there be some who know volumes of truth, but some will do great works of truth in God's name and still never really know God. How can this be?

What book of the Bible do people tend to avoid? The Book of Revelation. Contrary to popular belief, reading it will not give you nightmares. When people were asked to describe the last book of the Bible, the top five characteristics were: various beasts, the anti-Christ, Satan, hell, and the plagues. Read carefully and you will find that the total mentions are rare compared to how many times the book mentions "the Lamb". In fact, despite having only 22 chapters, the Book of Revelation refers to "the Lamb" over 30 times. The first words read, "The revelation of Jesus Christ" (Revelation 1:1, ESV). When Paul wrote, "I know whom I have believed," he simplified all the theological diatribes into one salient Someone!

As you negotiate all you have to do this week, begin and end with the Person of Christ. If you need a reminder, consider the faithful apostle Paul in his last moments. What started him on the journey was the person of Jesus and at the sunset of his life there was only one "Someone" who mattered.

INSIDE OUT

How is Jesus revealed in all the books of the Bible? Some examples are more obvious than others, but work through each book first from memory and write out how Jesus is revealed in that book at the beginning. For example, in the book of Daniel, Jesus is revealed as the fourth man in the fiery furnace and the Ancient of Days. In Exodus, Jesus is the Passover Lamb and the rock.

Read Hebrews 1:3 and reflect on the significance of the message for you today.

Sometimes noticing individual people amid the flurry of your "To Do List" is a way to cultivate a greater awareness of Christ. Identify some people who you want to give undivided attention to this week.

40. STAND FIRM MOVE FORWARD

"Therefore, my dear brothers and sisters, stand firm. Let nothing move you. Always give yourselves fully to the work of the Lord, because you know that your labor in the Lord is not in vain." (1 Corinthians 15:58)

Standing on the beach as the shallow waters of the ocean pour back into the deep, there is a noticeable "pull". So powerful is the movement of water over the land that you need to strengthen your stance against the momentum. Also, the forceful movement of the water erodes the sand under your feet, causing you to feel unbalanced. This wonder in the natural world also illustrates what happens to a believer's faith.

Have you ever had your deepest convictions pulled out to sea? Every believer should expect that their most resolute beliefs will be challenged by the natural order life on earth. Even though someone may arrive at certain convictions through heartfelt practice, there is no guarantee that those foundations won't be shaken. Like the ocean tide that undermines the ground on which you stand, the gravity of this world seeks to draw away Christian convictions with unrelenting effort. You may experience the occasional surprise wave that knocks you down, but more often it is the constant, more subtle pull of culture and the endless struggle of life that wears away your ability to stand firm.

Consider a few questions that convey examples of the gravitational pull today: What is the real point of following Christ? Is God really involved in human lives or do we see only what we want to see? Does anyone really know what happens when you die? How do I believe in something that really can't be proven by science? To what degree is the Bible able speak to the issues that are important to people today? Is there really a truth that is "the truth" that applies to all people, all places, and all times? Like the pull of the ocean under your feet, such questions seek to erode the basic assumptions you may have once stood firmly on. Perhaps it calls to mind the snake in the garden and the style of its approach when it asked Eve, "Did God really say, 'You must not eat from any tree in the garden'?" (Genesis 3:1).

This is not to say that questions are the enemy. Some will try to avoid questions thinking they will avoid the battle and "be safe," *but does it really work that way?* (Did you see what I did there?) If the Christian life on earth is in conflict with another way of life, then avoiding the questions only delays the inevitable. How do you stand firm when the tide pulls at you? One way to keep from falling over is to move. To assert your motion against the gravitational pull helps to keep you stable. Standing still makes you vulnerable, but moving up the beach, toward the land or even toward the water tends to make your balance more certain. In today's passage on conviction the Bible says, "Let nothing move you." How do you keep from getting "moved" in order to "stand firm"?

Strangely enough, the way to stand firm is not to stand still, but to move intentionally toward the goal. Paul urges believers who wish to "stand firm" to "always give yourselves fully to the work of the Lord". If you feel uncertain about relevance of the Bible, read it, live it, and see for yourself. Test the strength of the tide and intentionally profess your belief in the Creator and Savior of this world. "Do the work" and move purposefully for God and you will discover just how reliable your convictions are. Again, know that when the writers of the Bible repeat warnings and encouragements about "standing firm" it is because it's a struggle for those who would hear the message. Read a few reminders from the apostle to the New Testament church about standing firm: 1 Corinthians 15:1; Galatians 5:1; Philippians 1:27; 2 Thessalonians 2:15.

Finally, when this broken world urges you to wonder if God's truth is really real, read 1 Thessalonians 3:8, which boldly states, "For now we *really* live, since you are standing firm in the Lord." May you decide this week to stand firm in your faith by moving toward what God calls you to do.

INSIDE OUT

What Bible characters demonstrate a life of conviction that stands firm?

How do you see the world and the Christian faith continually challenging what is "real" versus what is "not real"?

Stand on one foot and try to keep your balance. Then practice walking on a curb keeping your balance as you move forward. Moving toward something is still more stable even though you are still only standing on one foot at a time.

41. A CALL TO SPUR ONE ANOTHER

"And let us consider how we may spur one another on toward love and good deeds, not giving up meeting together, as some are in the habit of doing, but encouraging one another—and all the more as you see the Day approaching." (Hebrews 10:24, 25)

When you think about the work of the Christian community, "spurring" is not typically listed as an effective method for promoting spiritual growth. One might spur a horse to provoke it to move forward or move faster, but it's not the sort of normal activity that is encouraged in churches. Spurring surprises and hurts, and until someone can speak and understand the equestrian language, it's safe to assume that horses would prefer not to be spurred. Speaking on behalf of the human race, most people tend to resist even the most well intended spurring from others. Generally, humans usually wish for motivators that are less sudden and preferably not as sharp. For example, one can safely say that spurring is not considered a "best practice" for courtship. Most would-be relationships are the result of wooing, not spurring.

Some might see the call to "spur one another" as an opportunity to rebuke people, tell them what they are doing wrong, and tell them what they should be doing instead. Such an approach simply does not produce love or good works. To spur really means to provoke or incite—to stir up. Why does the Bible urge believers to "consider how we may spur one another to love and good deeds"? Think about the context of this challenge. Starting from verse 19 the reader is gathered up in the momentum of our new standing with God because of the finished work of Christ. The words "us", "we", and "our" are used at least 8 times in the verses leading up to the part about "spurring" each other. We don't learn or experience salvation in isolation, but with and through the community of faith. In other words, the nature of spurring is clearly not coming from a critical person whipping Christian stragglers into shape, but a collective urging of "us" forward. Instead of "You need to do this!" it is more about "We should do this!"

Think of how you are incited, stirred up, or provoked to new attitudes and behaviors. Not all reminders are equal; badgering or nagging will produce very little love or good works. However, being reminded by someone else's good example has a way of waking people up to a better way. Because love is more vividly portrayed in actions than words or ideas, we spur each other by setting an example. Show instead of tell.

A potential student was visiting a college campus and noticed the president and several members of administration walking towards them. Suddenly, the president stopped and bent down to pick a paper cup that littered the walkway and carried it until he could find a trash can. You could see the sting of gentle rebuke on everyone's faces because they were not paying attention. Everyone walked by it, but only one saw it and led by example. Without a doubt, those fellow administrators who witnessed that simple act were "spurred" to do likewise.

Spurring each other well can only happen when "we" are together. Apparently, when faced with challenges, there were some who refused to gather to worship and fellowship with other believers, thus disengaging from the essence of what it means to be a church. Whatever problems a community of faith faces, distance and distraction are not the way to resolve them.

Finally, notice how spurring ends with encouragement? We build and bolster each other with words of encouragement. Maybe you can think of times when you were made stronger, sweeter, or more determined to persevere because of someone else's words.

As you approach this week there are three challenges to the Christian believer from Hebrews 10:24, 25:
1. Provoke each other to love and goods deeds—by doing them.
2. Relentlessly meet together, no matter how hard it is, because "we" will always be better than "me".
3. Freely say the words that will build people up according to the grace of God.

May the mercy of God and the power of His Spirit awaken in you a fire—a deep stirring of meaning and purpose as you become the church you are called to be.

INSIDE OUT

Of these three challenges, which is the most difficult for you? Which is more natural for you to do? Which of the three would change your life the most if you put it into practice today?

Read reflect on the following passages and choose a day or two to live out the words of Scripture.
- 1 John 3:18
- Romans 12:4-5
- Ephesians 4:29

42. ENDEAVOR TO PERSEVERE

"So do not throw away your confidence;
it will be richly rewarded. You need to
persevere so that when you have done the
will of God, you will receive what he has
promised." (Hebrews 10:35, 36)

*I*t is it is easier to stand adversity than to stand prosperity. Do you agree or disagree? Those who have endured a bit of suffering may say, "I'd like to try prosperity for a while and see for myself." In fact, there are some who don't necessarily wish for massive prosperity; just a simple reprieve from the trouble would be enough. However, it is true that the choices you make about what is good, right, and true will often lead you through times of trouble. Remember that convictions are not opinions or ideas that fly through our minds—they are earned, nursed, and refined in the struggle. It is also true that every core value gets challenged along the way. If you are human, you will experience some degree of conflict for your convictions. The believers hearing this letter were among those who had experienced serious persecution:

"Remember those earlier days after you had received the light, when you endured in a great conflict full of suffering. Sometimes you were publicly exposed to insult and persecution; at other times you stood side by side with those who were so treated. You suffered along with those in prison and joyfully accepted the confiscation of your property, because you knew that you yourselves had better and lasting possessions" (Hebrews 10:32-34).

To those who already had faced much, the message is: "Don't throw away your confidence." In other words, refuse the urge to quit before you make it to the end. Stay the course. Endure to the finish. Persevere. In what areas of your life do you need to persevere? In what way are you tempted to quit and throw away your confidence? Most people desire more of a middle ground or a grey area in life so they can cultivate a comfort zone of relief, not realizing that very zone is where many languish. For example, people travel to different parts of the world to holiday in a place that is warm, because warmth is relaxing. Freezing cold is unbearable and the infernal heat of the desert is oppressive, but warmth is nice. So the core value of desirable weather is an environment with as little adversity as possible.

Apply the same principle in another area of life. Consider how lying, cheating and stealing are ultimately a commitment to the "easy way out". If you don't want to work, steal. If owning your mistakes feels costly, lie. There is no happy medium, no balanced approach, no middle of the road effort in this passage we're going over right now. You are either throwing away that which has been real to you or you are pressing on toward a goal. Maybe this sounds a bit extreme, but maybe avoiding the extreme is part of the problem.

God's word is filled with the challenge to "persevere", along with real life stories of people displaying the virtue of perseverance, but very little is ever said about *how* to persevere. Maybe it's because perseverance is just one of those aspects of life you should not try to tease apart or over-analyze. Nothing is really gained by understanding more about why people suffer. Is saying, "Just press through this trial and you will see. Just hang on to your hope and get through the fog. You can assess the experience on the other side," just too simplistic? People who labor to understand every nuance of life rarely have the energy to live out that life that they have. Those who endeavor to persevere usually learn more about the meaning of the ups and downs after having made it through.

May the love of God strengthen you to finish well.

INSIDE OUT

This week, read and reflect on the nature and work of perseverance, as revealed in these passages: Luke 8:15; Romans 5:3–5; 1 Peter 1:6–9.

Scan through your memory of people we read about in the Bible who had to endure to the end in order to really know the journey was worth it. How do you relate to obstacles and adversity? Consider the people in your life who negotiate trials well and invite them to advise you and pray for you.

For years many have heralded the two characteristics of the remnant people at the end of time as having two qualities (Revelation 14:12 states that they keep the commandments and have the testimony of Jesus). More should be made of the "patient endurance" part of the story. Chances are high that today you face an obstacle in your journey that distracts you or seems to block your way with fear and uncertainty. Remember, perseverance is a by-product of practice. And sometimes it is solely a matter of walking all the way to the finish that determines winning in the end.

This week, reflect on the choices you have made that require you to endure to the end.

FULLY ASSURED

The question has often been asked, "If you were to die today, are you sure you would be saved?" Many have been encouraged not to answer "yea" or "nay" to this question. Perhaps one of the more difficult experiences of the Christian life is living with the assurance of salvation. While there certainly are dangers to mindlessly accepting the gift and taking it for granted, there's also dangers in living with a sense of fear that you no matter what you believe, you still may not pass the test. The Bible offers a powerful message of how reliable God is to do for you what you cannot do for yourself. If you struggle with uncertainty and long for a resolute confidence in your eternal home, this journey will strengthen your heart and your sense of hope.

43. KNOW IT ALL

"I write these things to you who believe in the name of the Son of God so that you may know that you have eternal life." (1 John 5:13)

Someone once said, "Knowledge is power." There are things to know that no one needs to know. Did you know that beetles taste a little like apples, wasps taste like pine nuts, and *almost* is the longest word in the English language with all the letters in alphabetical order? Did you know that in 1386, the French executed a pig by public hanging for the crime of murder? Some people on the planet don't know that a cockroach can live for several weeks with its head cut off, and right-handed people live, on average, nine years longer than left-handed people. Did you know that your fingernails grow four times faster than toenails and women blink nearly twice as often as men? Of course, most people don't know that some worms will eat themselves if they can't find food and the longest recorded flight of a chicken is thirteen seconds. Did you know that the technical term for the numbness when a part of your body goes to sleep is *obdormition?* Add to your mental trivia the not so well known truth that a rat can last longer without food than a camel, then ask yourself the question: "What will I do with my increased knowledge?" Clearly, you already *know* the answer. Not much.

Knowledge. A bright-eyed teacher might say to a student: "I know this is difficult for you now, but I also know it will be easy for you by the end of the week." Imagine the relief a patient feels when a medical doctor calmly says, "Take this medicine and you will feel better in the morning." Hope dawns on the anxious heart of a car owner when the automotive mechanic listens to the sound of the sputtering engine and states confidently, "It sounds like an exhaust leak; we will get it fixed in an hour." How does a seasoned grandmother patiently carry a screaming baby and softly coo words to the child that, in the moment, seem unimaginable? "You are so tired—it won't be long until you are asleep." She just knows.

There is a knowledge worth knowing. Of all that there is to know, knowing that you have eternal life might be the most crucial. How does one gain the conviction for the most precious of all endeavors? In Mark 10:17 a man asks of Jesus, "What must I do to inherit eternal life?" While some may become concerned about treading casually upon the gift of salvation with overconfidence, your eternal home is the "one thing" God would have us all be completely sure of. Some convictions are earned through hard work, investment, commitment, and sacrifice. Some convictions are stirred abruptly in the moment of an insight or a spiritual awakening. Still others sneak up on you over a lifetime and grow slow and solid like an oak tree. Being certain in the knowledge that today you are saved—safe from the power of sin and death is pivotal for everyone, but most especially for people in their young adult years.

How does one experience such an assurance? One way to become more confident of your salvation is to practice *reflecting* on the plan of salvation as it has been revealed to you. Practice *reminding* yourself of truths you know that can get drowned out by the storms of life. *Rejoice* out loud, in a song, writing concepts down on a page or in a journal, and declaring these words: "Because of the grace of God, I belong to Him, and I am going home one day." Whatever phrase or phrases you choose to use, the more you practice, the more it becomes real to you as you say it with joy. What you believe about eternal life changes the way you live your life here and now. Ask yourself the question: is what God has done for you enough to save you for eternity? What do you say? May the work God has done to give you eternal life be enough to give you peace today.

INSIDE OUT

How do you cultivate the assurance of salvation in your heart and mind? How do you become confident in your eternal home? Reflect on, remind yourself of, and rejoice in your eternal hope as you explore passages from the Bible on the assurance of salvation.

John 5:24; Romans 8:16; Hebrews 7:25; John 10:29; John 6:47; Romans 8:38, 39

Ask some of the people you know who are confident of their eternal life how and what they do to foster their sense of assurance.

44. SPEAK FREELY

"This is the confidence we have in approaching God: that if we ask anything according to his will, he hears us. And if we know that he hears us—whatever we ask—we know that we have what we asked of him."
(1 John 5:14, 15)

When you sit down, are you confident the chair will support you? Like clockwork, the sun moves from the east to the west. You inhale air, but you know not to try breathing water. If you were to drop a book, you know gravity will pull it to the ground. Seemingly fixed laws are all around, but ask any believer: "Are you confident that when you pray you will get whatever you ask for?" and you will discover that prayer is not one of those predictable principles of life. Even though you have the word of God urging you confidently into conversation with Him, the evidence of unanswered prayers is too great to ignore. When God doesn't heal the disease, or provide a job, or calm the raging storms in your life, you tend to wonder if you are being heard. And if He hears you—why doesn't He give you what you ask for?

If you are one of those super saints, and all your prayers get answered and you walk in intimate unity with God (perhaps like Enoch did), then keep walking on to another chapter and skip this section, because you will not understand. For those of you who need a confidence boost every once in a while, read on. To suggest that God will give you whatever you ask for is foundationally unrealistic. You may want a million dollars and you may ask for a million dollars, but most who do don't become millionaires. Nowhere in Scripture is God found acting like a wish-granting genie compelled to do whatever you ask. Why, then, are there so many examples in the Bible where Jesus seems to present His Father as being willing to give you what you want?

Read the context of all those statements and note that Jesus is offering unlimited resources to fit every need they will have *in order to complete God's will and His mission.* For example, in John 14:13 Jesus declares brazenly, "I will do whatever you ask in my name, so that the Father may be glorified in the Son. You may ask me for anything in my name, and I will do it." This is an untenable and crazy thing to say until you go back and read what led up to the declaration. Jesus basically prophesies that when the Holy Spirit comes on them, after His ascension, they will be up to their ears in gospel work: "Very truly I tell you, whoever believes in me will do the works I have been doing, and they will do even greater things than these, because I am going to the Father" (John 14:12). In other words, as they were filled with the Spirit, they would be doing God's will and His work. Everything, anything, whatever they needed for that work was promised to them.

John writes to the church reminding them to be confident about their standing with God as they pray. Like a fixed law, know that when you come to God the way is clear. Be confident that the truths you know are real, binding, and eternal. There are conditions, however, to the results of your praying. Essentially, are you praying for what you need to build God's kingdom? In other words, when you pray, are you asking God for what you want or are you willing to ask God for whatever He wants? The disciples had made such a step and although they did not understand all of the implications of their decision to follow Christ—they chose Jesus and His will, and later learned what it was all about.

Be confident that as you approach the task of doing God's will, whatever you need you will have.

INSIDE OUT

Some of the promises Jesus gave about prayer are qualified by certain conditions. Read and reflect on the following statements of Jesus and what it means for the community of faith.

John 14:13, 14; Matthew 18:19; Matthew 21:22

Consider this: Is it possible that in praying our hearts are not always in the right place or directed in the right way? (Isaiah 29:13; Matthew 15:8)

Sometimes we limit our confident conversation with God by choosing only the words we habitually use. When you pray this week, try praying *without* using any of the following words or phrases:
- "Dear Jesus"
- "Father in Heaven"
- "In Jesus's name, Amen"
- "Please be with"
- "Bless"
- "Forgive"
- "I pray"
- "Thank you for"
- "Send Your Holy Spirit"
- "Help me/us/them"

45. TIME-LAPSE CONVICTIONS

"In all my prayers for all of you, I always pray with joy because of your partnership in the gospel from the first day until now, being confident of this, that he who began a good work in you will carry it on to completion until the day of Christ Jesus." (Philippians 1:4-6)

Think about the all of the projects you started, but did not finish. Sometimes you may start and not finish because you lose interest, or the cost is greater than your resources. Of course, there are projects that become irrelevant over time. For example, one man set his goal of building a tree house for his kids, but over time his children grew up faster than he could complete the project, leaving a pile of wood and a great idea that lost its meaning.

Which best describes you?
   A. I will only do one project at a time and will not think of starting another one until the first is completed.
   B. I will have two or more projects laying around, part-way done or at least started, and I'll get them done when I have the opportunity.

Imagine if you were to put person A to work with person B on a task like building a house, cooking a meal for a large gathering, or beautifying a garden or yard. What do you think might happen? First there would be conflict, but you can also see how their differences could complement each other, if they valued one another.

What project is Paul referring to when he promises that, "He who began a good work in you will carry it on to completion…"? (Philippians 1:6) Often this verse describes the sanctifying work of God in people that will not be finished until Christ comes. If so, why would the loving apostle even need to share the words of promise and encouragement? Is it possible that some might be tempted to doubt God's effective work in their lives? Honestly, do you easily see unmistakable evidence of your own spiritual growth? It's rarely about questioning whether God is faithful or true, but more about you being a willing, active, and positive participant in your own growth process.

There is a good reason Paul writes to the Philippians about their growth as a sure thing, even confessing of himself, "I do not do the good I want to do, but the evil I do not want to do—this I keep on doing... What a wretched man I am! Who will rescue me from this body that is subject to death?" (Romans 7:19, 24). When you try to look at your own growth you just don't see it well, but when you look at others through eyes of confidence in God's will and His way, you see His unmistakable handiwork in people.

Growth is more visible in others than it will ever be looking at yourself. Also, hearing yourself say, "God's growing me" is one thing, but hearing someone else say with sincerity, "God is clearly making a difference in your life" is truly encouraging and heartwarming. In this well-known power promise from Scripture Paul does at least two things that are worth putting into practice this week: 1) He prays for God's work to be done in others, and 2) He tells others how God is visibly working in them.

If you want to know that God is working in you, shift your focus to how God is at work in others. Be specific. Be thoughtful. Be intentional in going out of your way to say it. Know that in the same way you have a hard time seeing your own growth, others might wonder how you see a change in them, but that's okay. They won't see the change you see. It is too incremental. Did you notice hit a growth spurt? Did you wake up one morning and feel like your limbs lengthened overnight? No, but when you are constantly aware of yourself, the growth is unnoticeable. When you look at someone else—from one occasion to another—you see the change.

INSIDE OUT

Make a list of the people you interact with on a regular basis and select a few to prayerfully think about how they are growing in God's grace. Sometimes simply offering an observation about a skill they are improving or a more mature attitude they possess will make an impact.
How does knowing that someone believes the best about you shape the way you live?

Consider the following passages about growth throughout the week and at the end, rank 3-5 selections as the most helpful to you.

2 Corinthians 9:10; Ephesians 4:16; Hebrews 5:12-14; James 1:4; Luke 8:14, 15; 2 Corinthians 13:9; Colossians 1:28; Colossians 1:10

46. ABOVE SEE LEVEL

"I have been crucified with Christ and I no longer live, but Christ lives in me. The life I now live in the body, I live by faith in the Son of God, who loved me and gave himself for me." (Galatians 2:20)

The deepest of all convictions are born not at our common line of sight, but by lifting our eyes beyond or above "see level". Think about how the creatures that live in the sea never see a tree or a snow-covered mountaintop, and therefore don't know another way of life. How is this also true of the world we live in? More than ever before, the world today needs a vision of Jesus Christ.

The word *Christ* is used frequently. An untold number of people claim the label "Christian". Jesus is a well-known historical figure. But there is more. Consider Lilias Trotter for a moment. Hers is not a household name, but her life inspired Helen Lemmel to write the song *Turn Your Eyes Upon Jesus*. Because of the simplicity and truth of the chorus, the song has a way of sticking in your mind and riding around in your memory for a while. Trotter was an accomplished artist who answered the call to put away her artistic endeavors and take up a life as a missionary to the Muslims in Algeria. Her faithful labor for 38 years produced an even more remarkable work of art in the sight of her Savior, Jesus Christ. Her passionate and resolute vision for Jesus illustrates a theme in Scripture that often gets overlooked.

The idea of what it means to be "in Christ" captures the very heart of what it means to be Christian. Take a brief journey through some of the more salient examples of the phrase "in Christ". There is really no need for commentary, explanation, or insights from an author, other than what has been written long ago.

In Ephesians 1:4 Paul declares that "God chose us *in Christ* before the foundation of the world," and later to Timothy echoes the same idea, saying, "He gave us grace *in Christ* Jesus before the ages began" (2 Timothy 1:9). It is true that "*In Christ* we have redemption through his blood, the forgiveness of our trespasses" (Ephesians 1:7). It is a well-known fact that, "The wages of sin is death, but the free gift of God is eternal life *in Christ* Jesus our Lord" (Romans 6:23). All this is possible because, "For our sake God made Christ to be sin who knew no sin, so that *in him* we might become the righteousness of God" (2 Corinthians 5:21).

What this means today is:
1. "If anyone is *in Christ,* he is a new creation. The old has passed away; behold, the new has come." (2 Corinthians 5:17)
2. *"In Christ* Jesus you are all sons of God, through faith." (Galatians 3:26)
3. "God raised us up with Christ and seated us with him in the heavenly places *in Christ* Jesus." (Ephesians 2:6)
4. "My God will supply every need of yours according to his riches in glory *in Christ* Jesus." (Philippians 4:19)

Oh, but that is not all—there is more. With unmistakable certainty the seasoned apostle states: "I am sure that neither death nor life, nor angels nor rulers, nor things present nor things to come, nor powers, nor height nor depth, nor anything else in all creation, will be able to separate us from the love of God *in Christ* Jesus our Lord" (Romans 8:38, 39).

The plan of salvation can be summed up by simply saying, "For as in Adam all die, so also *in Christ* shall all be made alive" (1 Corinthians 15:22) accompanied by the promise that "The peace of God, which surpasses all understanding, will guard your hearts and your minds *in Christ* Jesus" (Philippians 4:7). And if we have missed anything, answer any of the questions or fill in the blanks with the conviction that "All the promises of God find their Yes *in Christ"* (2 Corinthians 1:20). The phrase "in Christ" is not slang, nor is it a throwaway line to be used when you don't know what else to say. "In Christ" is the conviction that there is nothing more to see, know, believe, commit to, or live and die for.

Do you see? Do you see Jesus? May you by faith *in Christ* find the confidence to sing about the good news of being a believer *in Christ.*

INSIDE OUT

Make it a point to sing the song *Turn Your Eyes Upon Jesus.* Consider the simple, but life-changing promise of the words in the chorus.

If you have ever looked through a camera lens you will notice that when you focus on one object, the others things in the background get blurry. How is this true of what it means to elevate your "see" level?

This week, intentionally direct conversations that are negative, or discouraging, or cynical to the topic of Jesus.

47. THEME SONG

"Surely God is good to Israel..." (Psalm 73:1)

What is your favorite song? Some songs arrest you by the tune or the rhythm while other songs pull you into the message of the songwriter. If you enjoy music, you probably don't have one favorite song, but a favorite song for every category of music you listen to. Asaph is a songwriter in the Bible who sings a song that should top the music charts of history. Without even hearing the tune or knowing the musical genre, all you need to do is read Psalm 73 from beginning to end to be moved by the song. If there ever was a "theme song" for those who wrestle with their convictions, it is the song of Asaph in Psalm 73. Listen to Asaph's story in four movements.

Disillusion—*"Surely God is good to Israel, to those who are pure in heart. But..."* (Psalm 73:1). "God is good?" Surely you have been to events where the speaker wailed, "God is good!" and the congregation roared back, "All the time!" In a way, this is what Asaph says when he starts the song, however the next word in the song causes an abrupt shift, and the song that started out in glorious praise takes a surprising turn. In verses 2-12 Asaph sings of how the wicked are blessed and those who are righteous are afflicted. Like singing *Jesus Loves Me* or *God is So Good* then stopping immediately to say, "It's all wrong!" With this psalm Asaph sings about his confusion.

Dilemma—*"Surely in vain I have kept my heart pure and have washed my hands in innocence. All day long I have been afflicted, and every morning brings new punishments. If I had spoken out like that, I would have betrayed your children"* (Psalm 73:13-15). Likely, you have had seasons where adversity spins you around and makes you dizzy. The dilemma is obvious: the good guys are losing and the bad guys are winning and that is not supposed to be how the story goes. Although this God-fearing musician tries to makes sense of it all, he encounters a moment of writer's block and sings, "I don't know what to think!" Do you recognize the song? When in your life have you wondered if God's goodness closed shop and went on vacation when you needed it the most? Keep listening!

Discovery—*"When I tried to understand all this, it troubled me deeply till I entered the sanctuary of God; then I understood their final destiny"* (Psalm 73:16, 17). Something Asaph saw when he went into the sanctuary changed his tune. Did he examine the theological significance of the plan of salvation?

Absolutely! How else could you arrive at the conclusion he came to when he sings, "Then I understood their final destiny"? There is a reason you will never exhaust the "sanctuary message" during this life on earth: the plan was constructed on God's table in heaven (Hebrews 8:5; Exodus 25:9, 40; 26:30). Maybe "the truth" turned Asaph's song around, but the sanctuary is more than just altars, blood, and candlesticks. The tabernacle of God was where He promised to "be with His people" (Exodus 25:8). Clearly, the combination of unmistakable insight and the very presence of God moved the music toward a crescendo of glory.

Declaration—"Yet I am always with you; you hold me by my right hand. You guide me with your counsel, and afterward you will take me into glory" (Psalm 73:23, 24). The message of Asaph's song is: God's grip on you is sure even when your grip on God is feeble. Not only has the knowledge of God's presence and His plan brought Asaph through despair, this weathered priest sings of the matchless majesty of God. Do you remember what Asaph was crying about at the beginning of the psalm? The wealth of the wicked, the prosperity of evildoers, the material and worldly fame of those who love sin and despise God had preoccupied Asaph's mind. Yet by the end he declares, "Whom have I in heaven but You? And earth has nothing I desire besides you" (Psalm 73:25).

Songs come and go, but this psalm might be the theme song of the human struggle for conviction. It is intellectual, emotional, structured, surprising, and it moves from one season to the next.

INSIDE OUT

This week, continue reading and reflecting on the psalms of Asaph (Psalms 50, 73-83) and consider how the music of the sanctuary relates to the world you live in today. Also, because Psalm 73 captures so many of the thoughts and experiences of people today, pray for an opportunity to share this beautiful song with people you meet.

KINGDOM CONVICTIONS

As you make your way to the end of this book, hopefully your sense of conviction has been stirred and your confidence in God's word strengthened. Make no mistake, what convicts you today is not written in stone, but rather in your heart—which means it can grow or diminish. The final devotions in this section stem from a handful of sureties that are available to you today. As you will notice, the word "surely" is used often in scripture but the group of young adults who worked on this book have chosen the following as the most pressing convictions of which to be sure. Know that there is a home that waits for you that is more real than the ground under your feet or the air in your lungs. If God is all that you have come to believe He is, then you can count on the soon coming of Christ and a new day ahead.

48. LITTLE ONES

"He took a little child whom he placed among them. Taking the child in his arms, he said to them, 'Whoever welcomes one of these little children in my name welcomes me; and whoever welcomes me does not welcome me but the one who sent me.'" (Mark 9:36, 37)

L ook at the life of Christ and see what stirs the deep emotions of Jesus as He interacts with people. For those who are helpless, Jesus feels compassion. For those who are ambassadors of great faith, Jesus is amazed! For those who misuse, mistreat, or simply miss the significance of even "the least of these," Jesus gets angry—indignant. When you are preoccupied with your own sense of self-importance, everyone around you dwarfs in comparison. Jesus rebuked the selfish ambitions of His crew on more than one occasion, sometimes with vivid illustrations, such as the unmitigated simplicity of a child.

"He placed a child among them." While children are innocent and heartwarming, they cannot advance your station in life or provide you anything of material value. Kids need older people. Adults must do things for children in order for them to survive and grow, so why would Jesus equate welcoming Him with welcoming a child? What did Jesus mean to say when He placed a child in front of the disciples saying, "This is how I want to you to be!"? Maybe Jesus tried to convey that when you invite the poor and the seemingly "unimportant" people into your life, it's like opening your arms to God Himself. And if you didn't get it by listening to Jesus, the Son of God illustrates one of His deepest convictions by simply "taking a child in His arms" as He spoke.

If you were to practice such an attitude toward the "least of these," what might be different about your day? It's likely that more than your day would be different; it could change your life! "If anyone causes one of these little ones—those who believe in me—to stumble, it would be better for them if a large millstone were hung around their neck and they were thrown into the sea" (Mark 9:42). Jesus clears away any confusion as to how He feels about people who trip up the little ones in their faith and it's simply this: don't mess with the children. Why such a visceral response? *If you don't learn to value the people in life who cannot doing anything for you, then you don't really understand the nature of God's grace.*

Test the principle out yourself: Show kindness to someone who has nothing to offer you in return and in doing so you will experience the kindness God delivers to humanity. Again, later in the gospel of Mark, the disciples prevent kids from coming to Jesus because it is unseemly for the Rabbi to be pestered by such "little people". By now you can imagine why Jesus became "indignant" and said to His disciples, "'Let the little children come to me, and do not hinder them, for the kingdom of God belongs to such as these. Truly I tell you, anyone who will not receive the kingdom of God like a little child will never enter it.' And he took the children in his arms, placed his hands on them and blessed them" (Mark 10:13-15).

The caution and the calling for those living under the convictions of God's Kingdom are clear:
1. Go the extra mile to make life better for the little ones of the world.
2. Make sure you are a conduit to God's grace and not an obstacle.

It will always be easier to curry favor with those who are influential. It will always be easier to ignore the noisy cries of those who are not great in the eyes of the world. It will always be easier to find a nobler or more deserving candidate for your kindness, but you are not called to "easy". Convictions that run deep in the kingdom of God are not "easy". You can wait for the opportunity of helping the helpless to be more convenient, or you can choose the kingdom way of seeing people in your life today. May the same grace that bought your ticket on the train bound for glory be made available to a "little one" through your kindness.

INSIDE OUT

Read the parable in Matthew 25:31-45 and practice an act of kindness to each of the "least of these" mentioned in the parable: hungry, thirsty, lonely, sick, and those who are imprisoned. There are a lot of ways to be hungry, thirsty, and in prison—think about it and bring a friend along as you seek out the best way for the little ones in life.

49. LITTLE THINGS

"Truly I tell you, anyone who gives you a cup of water in my name because you belong to the Messiah will certainly not lose their reward." (Mark 9:41)

It is to be noted how simple and seemingly small an act of kindness can be. If you are human, you may tend to envision a greater service, a more meaningful gift, or a much broader sphere of influence. Why give one Bible study when you can project a satellite message to millions? You can answer that question, but before you do—consider a few key details in the text above, and then survey how God uses the little things in life.

If *"anyone"* can do something as simple as offering water, then the challenge is not about being gifted, skilled or being a person of influence. The challenge then is: will you simply do or give what you can now? Taking it a step further, Jesus adds to the act of kindness the phrase, "in my name". Some try to hide the fact that they are Christians when they help others because they don't want to offend or alienate the ones they serve. Christ would say, "Do these things in my name and let me handle their perceptions." Finally, there is a reward. Something (perhaps better said, Someone) is motivating our acts of goodness. Throughout the four gospels Jesus describes the "reward" of His kingdom at least fifteen times! Maybe the greatest reward for offering a cup of cool water is that you finally feel at home in your skin. Young people often report that their greatest spiritual moments are the times they spend themselves in service to others.

Little people. In the previous chapter little people (by age, size, or position in life) are the chosen ones who display the grace of God to the world. Who fought and killed Goliath? David was the least likely to be chosen, the littlest boy of a family that was part of the smallest tribe of Israel. Who gave birth to Moses? Jochebed, a slave in Egypt. Who showed Naaman, the great Syrian captain, the way to find healing from leprosy? An unnamed girl who served as a maid. According to Jesus, who wins the prize for being the all-time greatest giver to the temple offering? An old widow who gave two mites! According to God, there are no little people.

Little places. Revivals occur in giant auditoriums or stadiums and historic events get displayed on the web or T.V., but God uses the little spaces to achieve the greatest work. The most famous meal recorded in the New Testament is held in a tiny upper room—a guest room at the top of someone's house. Where did the Holy Spirit come upon the waiting church fifty days after the resurrection? That same upper room. Where were most of the epistles written from? Likely, a small prison cell. According to God, there are no little spaces.

Little things. How did Jesus feed over five thousand people? He began with a small lunch basket from a little boy. What secret weapon did Shamgar use to slay six hundred enemies of God? An ox-goad became the warrior's weapon of choice. What newly discovered medicine did Jesus use to heal a man's blindness? A careful combination of three substances—spit, dirt, and water. With God, there are no little things.

Little tasks. For every Sermon on the Mount there is a Bible study at midnight with a cautious seeker, like Nicodemus. For every glorious display of glory, as on the mount of transfiguration, there are dozens of walks around the countryside with a small band of believers. For every temple cleansing and crowd gathering event, there are those precious one on one encounters with an outcast woman at a well or an appointment with Nathanael under a tree. After cancelling the threat of death, the resurrected Lord did not task Himself with reappearing in the court of Pilate or show up to harass Herod's court. Instead, Jesus took a 7-mile hike with two struggling disciples. Make no mistake, with God, there are no little tasks.

May you recognize and respond to the simple opportunities in your life this week.

INSIDE OUT

For each this week, focus your kindness on four different spheres of ministry: little people, little places, little things, and little tasks. Discuss with friends and fellow believers the question: in which sphere is it easier for you to serve and which do you find more difficult?

Read and reflect on the followings passages this week.
- 1 John 3:18
- 1 Corinthians 1:27
- Psalm 8:2
- Galatians 6:10
- James 1:27

50. SURELY

"And when the centurion, who stood there in front of Jesus, saw how he died, he said, 'Surely this man was the Son of God!'"
(Mark 15:39)

Today is likely to be an ordinary day for you—a day which is part of a normal week. Maybe today you will go to work, or school, or stay home and take care things that are your responsibility. Before you begin this day, consider three stories of unnamed people that went to work one ordinary Friday—a normal day when everything changed.

When the soldiers crucified Jesus, they took his clothes, dividing them into four shares, one for each of them, with the undergarment remaining. This garment was seamless, woven in one piece from top to bottom. "Let's not tear it," they said to one another. "Let's decide by lot who will get it." (John 19:23, 24)

There were commonly five pieces of clothing a person in that day would wear: sandals, an outer covering, a tunic, head covering or turban, and an inner covering or undergarment. Several decades after Jesus died and rose from the grave the apostle John includes this detailed inventory of how many items Jesus wore the day He died. The seamless undergarment of linen was the fifth piece out of four, and four soldiers assumed the rights to His clothing. Note the irony. The soldiers mock, mangle, and degrade the body of Jesus with causal indifference, while they protect his garment from being torn because the seamless piece of linen is valuable. The soldiers were just being soldiers, but they failed to see something more priceless than a piece of cloth. As they huddled around to cast lots for the piece of clothing, they turned their backs on something infinitely more valuable.

"The soldiers therefore came and broke the legs of the first man who had been crucified with Jesus, and then those of the other. But when they came to Jesus and found that he was already dead, they did not break his legs. Instead, one of the soldiers pierced Jesus' side with a spear, bringing a sudden flow of blood and water. The man who saw it has given testimony, and his testimony is true. He knows that he tells the truth, and he testifies so that you also may believe." (John 19:32-35)

Perhaps these soldiers were the same ones that now owned a few new articles of clothing as a bonus for their work. The text says they "found that he was already dead". Do you wonder why they would run a spear into Jesus when He was already dead? Perhaps they were uncertain and did not want to fail to do their job, so they were being conscientious. Why would someone do this? When the blood and water poured out, did it confirm His death in their minds? Did the soldier later connect how blood and water are the two emblems used to symbolize how Christians pass from death to life? Water, in the rebirth of baptism and blood in the cup of communion.

"And when the centurion, who stood there in front of Jesus, saw how he died, he said, 'Surely this man was the Son of God!'" (Mark 15:39) At the cross, who stays to bear witness? At the highpoint of Jesus's tragic demise, a lone Centurion utters a testimony so unimaginable every citizen would have to consider it. Even among those who were close disciples were confused, bewildered, and broken by the events of the cross, but the executioner is "sure". How is it that the Jews couldn't see their outrageous hypocrisy? How could so many people be so wrong about Jesus? What is more, how is it that one Roman soldier, with blood still on His hands, stands in the shadow of the cross and sees Jesus for who He really is?

"To be sure" is a dangerous testimony today. Some will brand you as unintelligent if you profess certainty. Others may call you "closed-minded". Still others in this life are looking for solid ground on which to stand. As you make your way into this "today" know that God is real today. The Cross happened right in the middle of someone's "today". Surely.

INSIDE OUT

This week practice seizing the day. At the end of each day, write two lists on one page. On one side write all the things that you did that day. On the other side write the things you know that God did. It takes a little practice, but as you begin to purposefully think about how real God is in each "today", the surer you will become of His goodness and grace.

The following passages echo the call to pay careful attention to the moments you have today.
- Psalm 118:24
- Ephesians 5:15-16
- Colossians 4:5-6
- Hebrews 3:13
- Hebrews 3:7
- Psalms 95:7-11

51. THE SURE WORD

"And the LORD God commanded the man,
'You are free to eat from any tree in the
garden; but you must not eat from the tree
of the knowledge of good and evil, for when
you eat from it you will certainly [surely] die.'"
(Genesis 2:16, 17)

God said you would surely die—the snake said you will not die. Who do you believe? Let's not complicate the issue with too many nuances and variables. God is either absolutely right, or trust the words of the snake—but you can't fully trust both. A popular saying goes like this: "There are two sure things in life: there is a God, and you are not Him." While this may seem like an obvious truth to you, the first and one enduring temptation for humanity is to distrust the "sure word of God". Do you remember Satan's temptations of Jesus, right after God had declared, "This is my Son!"? The evil one follows Jesus in to the desert saying, "If you are the Son of God, turn these stones to bread…" (Matthew 4:3).

At some point you must decide whether you will trust the word of God over your impressions and insights. Like stepping up on the rungs of a ladder, you can press your weight gently, slowly, and carefully or you can stomp the full force of your weight without a hesitation—the act of faith has a range expressions. Ultimately, you will have to place the full force of your weight on God's word to "verify" whether it's true. Furthermore, some leaps of faith will only be verified fully when it's too late to change your mind. Consider three sure promises that you will have to completely trust without verification.

Promise #1 "Go into all the world and make disciples and teaching them to obey everything I have commanded you. And *surely I am with you always, to the very end of the age*" (Matthew 28:20). *Commit all your resources to bringing the good news to the world, and I'll be with you all the way to the end.* What a promise! Of course, you have to endure to the end to verify whether His word is true. There is no other way than to fully trust God's word. You cannot make a disciple for Jesus by proclaiming, "I'm not sure about this Jesus, but I'm not sure about anything else, so just pick Jesus and see how it all turns out!" That is simply not worth the risk or the work and will not inspire anyone.

Promise #2 "He who testifies to these things says, 'Yes (surely), I am coming soon'" (Revelation 22:20). Maranatha! Jesus is coming! However, if the second coming of Jesus is only something you *hope* will happen and you only live as though it *may* happen, then you may be disappointed in the end. Jesus tells a number of parables that describe the "take it or leave it" approach to His return. God is definitely coming, but by the time Jesus shows up in the clouds of glory it will be entirely too late to say, "Okay, now I believe it!"

Promise #3 "'As surely as I live,' says the Lord, 'every knee will bow before me; every tongue will acknowledge God'" (Romans 14:11). Ultimately, everyone born of a woman (plus Adam and Eve) will admit that God is God and that He is righteous. So the notion that "all roads lead to the same heavenly home" is inaccurate, according to the Bible. All roads do lead to the place where everyone acknowledges that God is right and just. Whether you are saved or lost, you will ultimately agree.

These promises call for extreme faith. Outrageous trust. Uncommon confidence. Uncompromising resolve. And as you make your way home, these convictions will grow in you every step of the way.

INSIDE OUT

Which of the three promises is especially difficult for you? Why?

This week read 2 Peter 3 and reflect on Peter's final convictions before his life ended.

Think about some of the greatest Bible heroes who have wrestled with doubting God's word. Moses struck the rock when he was told to speak to the rock. Elijah hid in a cave after the letdown of mighty Mt. Carmel. Gideon shies away from the call to lead. All of these people survived the challenge to believe that God's word is sure and trustworthy, but not without a struggle. Maybe you know what God has said, but you also know what you have experienced, and sometimes God's word and your experience seem to disagree. As you hang on to God in those moments, your conviction strengthens you learn how reliable God's word is.

52. GOING HOME

"Surely your goodness and love will follow me all the days of my life, and I will dwell in the house of the LORD forever."
(Psalm 23:6)

If it is true that the season of young adulthood is a time to understand, embrace, and even express the convictions that have carved deep grooves in your heart, then know your journey has borne fruit that will last. What is the nature of the heart? What does it mean to be human? How do you come to convictions? What are the convictions explicit in Jesus, as well as others in the Bible? How do you become more confident in your beliefs? Of what can you be sure?

One thing is sure, you are not done. We are not done. In fact, from what you have considered in this book, there are many different directions to launch out, but it is time to land. Know that all the topics and themes— even the passages for these devotions were all chosen by young people 18-30 years of age. Also, know that "Going Home" seemed like the best to end. And so, consider the words of a shepherd about a Good Shepherd. In order to appreciate the 23 Psalm, you need to step into the sandals of a shepherd as they think about making their way home at the end of the day. David sings of two realities that conclude his song: 1) Something follows him home, and 2) Someone waits for him at home.

Maybe you have walked alone in the dark, whether in the city or in the country, it is difficult to not imagine that something is following you. Shepherds would be keenly aware of the wolves that would dog the steps of the shepherd and the flock. Yet, instead of a wolf or a lion, David hears the footsteps of "goodness" and "mercy" following him home. If you "know" that death is conquered and "nothing can separate you from God, how should you walk. What would it be like if believers of God's church heard only, saw only, loved only "goodness" and "mercy"?

In addition to what follows you home, there is what waits for you at home. Again, the Christian hope is not a doctrine or an experience, it is a Someone. The song David sings ends the same way the whole story ends: "And I will dwell in the house of Lord, all my days."

Did David mean the sanctuary? The palace? Did he mean the new earth? Listen to a few of David's other songs and maybe you will get an idea:

"One thing I have asked from the LORD, that I shall seek: That I may dwell in the house of the LORD all the days of my life, to behold the beauty of the LORD And to meditate in His temple." (Psalm 27:4)

"LORD, I love the house where you live, the place where your glory dwells." (Psalm 26:8)

"How blessed are those who dwell in Your house! They are ever praising You. Better is one day in your courts than a thousand elsewhere; I would rather be a doorkeeper in the house of my God than dwell in the tents of the wicked." (Psalm 84:4,10)

It has been said before in this book, but it seems appropriate to repeat it at the end: The Bible begins and ends with home. In Eden, the first family dwelt with God in intimate communion until the home was broken. You can say "we all come from a broken home." While most of the story is focused on what happens in the meantime, the beginning and end ought to be written in your heart.

"And I heard a loud voice from the throne saying, "Look! God's dwelling place is now among the people, and he will dwell with them. They will be his people, and God himself will be with them and be their God." (Revelation 21:3)

When you lose foundational reference points, it's easy to get lost or confused, distracted, and even disillusioned. So, anchor in to truth of Eden and sure promise of The New Earth. "I will dwell in the house of the LORD..." The surety of David's eternal home is heartwarming, and a relief. Because David's life is filled with both glorious moments of heroic faith and a few dark chapters of despicable brokenness, whatever your storied life has been, you too can go home.

In fact, make the choice today to say it more. If any theme should dominate the talk of church people today it is that we are headed home to be with God.

INSIDE OUT

This week work on a writing project. Spend the time to think about it, then write out your five deepest convictions. Use the most descriptive words possible and talk about them with others.